COMPLETE BOOK OF

Drills for Winning Basketball

Ken Lumsden

PRENTICE HALL
Paramus, NJ 07652

Library of Congress Cataloging-in-Publication Data

Lumsden, Ken.
 Complete book of drills for winning basketball: 245 easy-to-use
drills to put new variety and challenge into your practices and develop players' individual and team skills! / by Ken Lumsden.
 p. cm.
 ISBN 0-13-082979-X (spiral wire) ISBN 0-13-092575-6 (paper)
 1. Basketball--Training. I. Title.
GV885.35.L85 1999   98-28756
796.323--dc21   CIP

© 1999 *by* Prentice Hall

Acquisitions Editor: *Connie Kallback*
Production Editor: *Tom Curtin*
Interior Design/Formatting: *Dee Coroneos*

Every effort has been made to ensure that no copyrighted material has been used
without permission. The author regrets any oversights that may have occurred and
would be happy to rectify them in future printings of this book.

Printed in the United States of America

10 9 8 7 6 5 4 3   *10 9 8 7 6 5*

ISBN 0-13-082979-X (spiral wire)   ISBN 0-13-092575-6 (paper)

PRENTICE HALL
Paramus, NJ 07652

DEDICATION

I would like to dedicate this book to my wife, Elaine, and son, Chris, for all of their encouragement and support. They are the driving force behind many of my accomplishments.

ABOUT THE AUTHOR

Ken Lumsden has been a secondary physical education teacher and coach at Ashland Middle School in Ashland, Oregon, since 1976. He received his Master's degree in Physical Education and Health from Southern Oregon University in 1981. Ken's physical education curriculum book, *Ready-to-Use P.E. Activities and Tournaments for Grades 6-12*, co-authored with Sally Jones, was published by Parker, A Prentice Hall imprint, in 1996. He has also had articles published in two national journals, been a guest lecturer for college methods classes, and spoken at both state and national level physical education conferences. He has also created several games, a unique method of organizing students, and a procedure for success-oriented grading.

Ken is experienced as both a player and coach, having played basketball in high school, college, and in the military. He has coached for 24 years; held basketball coaching positions in middle school, junior high, high school and college; and coached football, baseball, volleyball, and track and field.

Ken and Elaine, his wife of 27 years, have one son, Chris. In his spare time, Ken is a Coast Guard licensed fishing guide, enjoys agate hunting, and develops inventions.

ABOUT THIS RESOURCE

The purpose of this resource is to present numerous ways to enhance any basketball program or practice. It is filled with drills, organizational plans, tournaments, simple statistics, skill testing, and other ready-to-use forms to facilitate most of the skill development phases of the game and should prove to be a valuable asset and resource for coaches, physical education instructors, and players.

The 245 easy-to-scan drills were designed to put spark and challenge into practice while genuinely helping players develop skills they need to work on individually or as a team. Presented one per page for coaches to understand at a glance, the drills make the reinforcement of any skill simpler by using a variety of techniques, styles, and strategies in ball handling and are motivational because they keep players moving and challenged at all times. The following description should give you an idea of what each section contains:

The first section presents several ideas that a coach or player should be aware of in order to optimize skill drill instruction and development. It covers concerns about safety, how to ensure success for everyone, and ways to maximize participation.

The second section deals with a method for wisely using the span of time prior to organized practice. Most players are just hanging out, shooting around, or working on the areas where they are already competent. When this time is added up over the course of the season, it translates into several hours. This is time that could and should be used to benefit all. A simple solution is prescribed.

Sections 3 through 11 present 245 drills that can be used to build upon the various proficiencies of basketball. They present a multitude of drills for conditioning, defense, dribbling, foul shooting, games, offense, passing, rebounding, and shooting. Each drill follows a similar format that includes the primary skill being taught, objective, equipment needed, coaching tips to players, procedure, options, and floor plan. The text is short, simple, and to the point. The diagrams are clear and easy to interpret. Each drill can be altered, changed, or adjusted to allow success for the varying degrees of ability within individuals or teams. Section 7, alone, offers a variety of more than twenty different games. Use them as incentives to end practice, as competitive challenges, or as tools for determining where additional work and refinement may be needed.

A simple method to record and keep statistics is the focus of section 12. It describes an uncomplicated, yet effective method for administering this crucial area. User-friendly forms and instructions are also provided.

Skill testing is described in section 13. It features both criteria and forms to place players on one level or another. The data provided should make those tough decisions and the rationale for selection or placement much easier.

The 14th section deals with how to introduce tournament play into a basketball program or practice. Spicing up a practice by including a round robin tournament adds competition, cooperation, and the desire to win. The section is complete with easy-to-understand instructions and reproducible forms.

The last section contains valuable forms that coaches will find useful for starting a file, creating play books, or visually explaining pertinent team information. These, too, are easy to use and simple to reproduce.

The use of this valuable resource can help coaches and players alike to realize a surge in excitement, motivation, and achievement. I sincerely hope that each player, coach, and program will become more successful. That is, after all, the primary objective.

Good luck and enjoy the results.

Ken Lumsden

Key to Symbols

Basketball =

Offensive player with the ball =

Offensive player = Ⓞ or ①

Defensive player = X   or X₂

Coach = Coach

Cone = Ⓒ

Path of a player = ——— 1 ———▶

Path of a dribbler = ⌇⌇⌇ 1 ⌇⌇⌇▶

First pass = ······· 1 ·······➤

Second pass = ········· 2 ·········➤

Screen or block set by a player = ——— 1 ———|

CONTENTS

5 DRIBBLING. 79

8 OFFENSE 157

10 REBOUNDING. 225

11 SHOOTING 251

METHODS FOR OPTIMIZING PRACTICE

*I have heard it said that the first ingredient of success—
the earliest spark in the dreaming youth—is this:
Dream a great dream.*

—John Alan Appleman

METHODS FOR OPTIMIZING PRACTICE

Listed below are some guidelines to help you get the most out of your basketball practices and drills. These should ensure that all participants will experience a safe and successful workout.

Create a Safe Environment

- Determine if the area is safe and free from obstacles.
- Make sure the floor is clean and dry.
- Discourage athletes from participating in running shoes, which usually position the heel higher than flat-soled basketball shoes. Because of this, when making quick stops or turns, the ankle may give way and sprain much easier.
- Monitor fatigue in the athletes and always provide plenty of liquid for fast and immediate consumption.
- Always discuss safety concerns when a drill requires it.
- Keep a medical kit stocked and nearby.

Ensure Success for Everyone

- Collect and keep on file any good drills that work for your program. Ask the players what they like or dislike about a given drill. Often times, player input is very valuable and can bring about positive changes too.
- Deploy new drills often. This habit will create interest and excitement, decrease player boredom, and give the athletes numerous methods for learning a skill.
- Evaluate each drill to determine if it is much too difficult for the intended age group. Bad habits can be developed when younger players are asked to do difficult or arduous tasks.
- Be creative! Take a risk and try something new on occasion. An example would be to play a timed game where the players may shoot, pass, and dribble with only their off hand. How about letting the team or various players be in charge of organizing and running a drill or even the entire practice once a month?
- Remember that by altering rules, shifting boundaries, changing distances, decreasing players, revamping scoring, redoing travel methods, and adjusting duration, coaches can make a drill become successful for almost any participant.

Maximize Participation

- Remember this for skill growth, "Improvement requires movement." How many times have you seen a coach set up two lines, one for lay-ins and the other for rebounding? A player dribbles in for a lay-in, then goes and stands in line a long

3

time. The other line gets the rebound, and they too stand in line before doing anything constructive. As visualized, there is very little improvement going on when only two people are actively participating.

➡ When using lines, keep the line as small as possible by duplicating the drill at another basket. This drastically reduces standing time.

➡ Whenever possible, give each player a ball for skill improvement drills.

➡ Keep everyone moving by adding different skills within one drill. An example of this is "Rattlesnake" in the offensive section. This also reduces standing down-time.

➡ Use every basket available for skill improvement drills. The more times players are allowed to perform a skill, the faster they will improve.

➡ Make sure that relay teams are very small in number. Three is usually the maximum. This will create more teams and give everyone extra opportunities to be involved. Dribbling down the court and back, then sitting while five other teammates do the same, is not the best or fastest way to reach a desired outcome.

➡ When participants are eliminated in drills or contests, either have them go elsewhere and practice, or allow them to remit after a certain amount of time.

➡ Playing games with fewer individuals will create more opportunities for everyone to experience movement, improvement, and success.

Section 2

BEFORE-PRACTICE BASKETBALL CIRCUIT

*Content yourself with doing;
let others do the taking.*

—Anonymous

BEFORE-PRACTICE BASKETBALL CIRCUIT

Coaches usually begin their organized practice each day at a set time. Most of the players are on the floor 10 to 15 minutes prior to the start. Usually, the athletes' accomplishments during this time are minimal because of the unstructured format. For some players, this is as high as 15 to 20 minutes of just shooting around. These before-practice periods, added up, will total several hours over the entire season. This time can and should be used wisely.

Developing a Before-Practice Circuit

This circuit was developed to put this precious time to use so that everyone can profit. The players benefit through practicing basic basketball skills, day after day. This allows positive skill reinforcement and skill foundation building. The coach is rewarded by having to spend less time on skill drills and is now allowed more time for the other significant aspects of the game.

The trainer or coach sets up the circuit and signals the time intervals. All stations last for one minute. A player may start anywhere. The players must stay in numerical order when rotating from station to station. If they do not, chaos will follow and mess up the whole rotation process by causing others to miss spots. All stations are numbered and the skill instructions for that specific area are written and posted. Only one player is allowed at each station. A coach may substitute new drills at any location. It is a good idea to change at least two or three drills each week so that player boredom does not become a problem.

SAMPLE DESCRIPTION OF THE DRILLS

Listed below are a few examples of fundamental drills that may be used at the established stations.

1. *Ball handling:* With or without gloves, circle the ball around the body then perform figure eights between the legs.

2. *Shooting:* Try right- and left-handed bank shots from five feet away.

3. *Passing:* Make behind-back passes against the wall from 10 to 15 feet away.

4. *Jumping:* Jump as high as possible 25 times against the wall. Alternate the right hand and left hand each jump.

5. *Rebounding:* Tip the ball against the backboard three times. On the fourth tip, direct the ball into the basket for a score.

6. *Dribbling:* Dribble through and around a line of cones or obstacles. Gloves and glasses may be used.

7. *Shooting:* Shoot five bank shots from the right side and then five bank shots from the left side from 8 to 10 feet away.

8. *Defense:* Slide from one chair to another while maintaining the proper defensive stance. The chairs are from 12 to 15 feet apart.

9. *Passing:* Using various techniques, pass against the wall from 10 to 15 feet. Masking tape targets may be added to improve passing accuracy.

10. *Shooting:* Shoot foul shots for the duration.

11. *Jumping:* Jump rope for the duration of time.

12. *Dribbling:* Dribble the ball behind the back and amidst the legs.

13. *Shooting:* Use your weak shooting arm from various spots.

14. *Shooting and rebounding:* Shoot a jump shot and immediately follow the shot for a rebound.

15. *Choice:* Players may choose any skill or activity to work on.

BEFORE-PRACTICE BASKETBALL
CIRCUIT FLOOR DIAGRAM

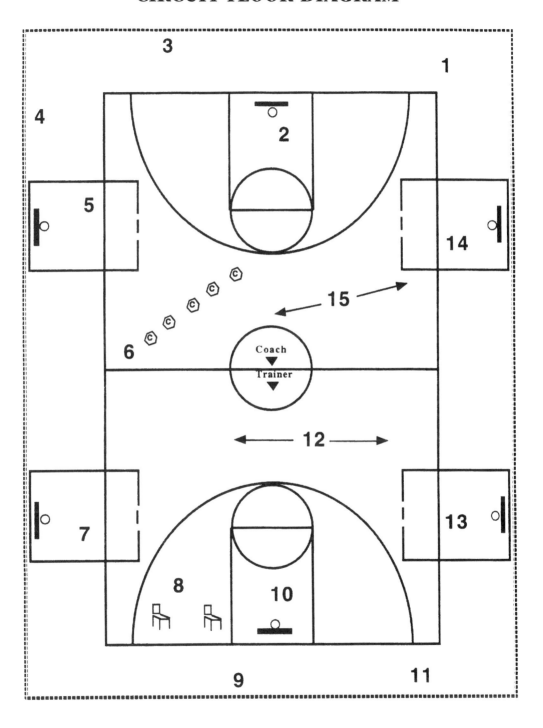

Section 3

CONDITIONING

*I find that the harder I work,
the more luck I seem to have.*

—Thomas Jefferson

AGILITY SPRINTS

Primary Skill: Conditioning

Objective: To develop agility and endurance.

Equipment Needed: None.

Coaching Tips to Players:
This is not a race. Do the steps correctly.

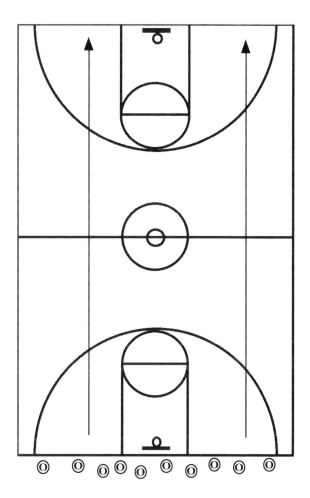

Procedure:

- Players line up on the end line.
- The coach specifies which step the players will implement to the other end.
- Use the following steps:
    a. Sprint.
    b. Run backwards.
    c. Frog hops.
    d. Hop five times with the left foot then five times with the right foot.
    e. Sprint and turn three full circles during the run.
    f. Slide sideways.
    g. Skip.
    h. Gallop.
    i. Jog.

ARMY

Primary Skill: Conditioning

Objective: To develop defensive fitness and proper foot movement.

Equipment Needed: None.

Coaching Tips to Players: Make rapid but controlled directional changes.

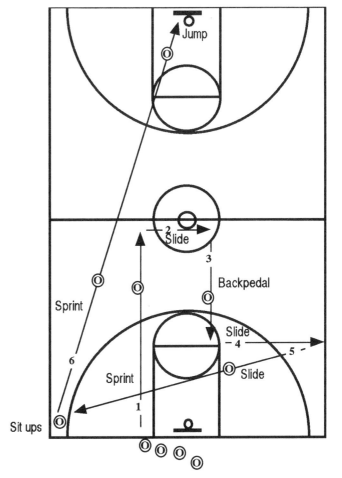

Procedure:

- Players form one line under the basket.
- A player will always face the far end of the court.
- As soon as a player touches half court, the next one begins.
- Apply the following skills and techniques:
    a. Sprint to half court and touch the floor.
    b. Defensive slide to the far side of the center circle and touch the floor.
    c. Backpedal to the foul line and touch it.
    d. Defensive slide to the side of the court and make contact with the side line.
    e. Defensive slide to the opposite lower corner and do five sit-ups.
    f. Sprint to the opposite basket and attempt to touch the net or rim five times.
- After all of the players have finished, begin again from the opposite end.
- Continue this drill a predetermined number of times.

BALL CIRCLES

Primary Skill: Conditioning

Objective: To develop hand and eye coordination.

Equipment Needed: One ball for each player.

Coaching Tips to Players: Concentrate.

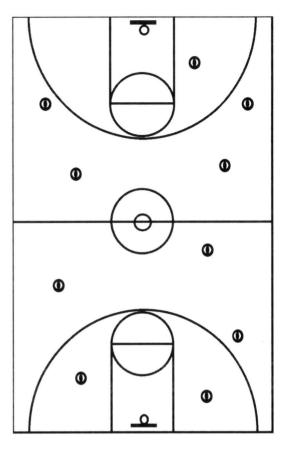

Procedure:

- Each player has a ball.
- Players spread out on a basketball court and do the following:
  a. Circle the ball clockwise around the right leg a predetermined number of revolutions. Reverse the ball and repeat the skill.
  b. Circle the ball around the left leg a projected number of times. Repeat the skill in the opposite direction.
  c. Circle the ball clockwise around both legs. Players will start at the feet, work up to the arm pits, and then back down. Reverse directions when the task is completed.
  d. Implement figure eights between and around the legs ten times. Reverse directions and repeat the skill.
  e. Using the above skills or movements created by players, implement a routine that constantly keeps the ball moving around the body for one minute.

BLAST OFF

Primary Skill: Conditioning

Objective: To develop cardiovascular endurance.

Equipment Needed: Four floor cones and one stopwatch.

Coaching Tips to Players: Work extra hard when passing the other players.

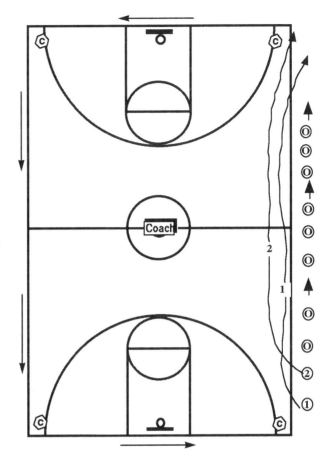

Procedure:

- All players line up in single file.
- Establish spacing of three to four feet apart.
- The entire group will jog around the perimeter of the basketball court. Be sure to stay outside the cones.
- O1 sprints by the whole group, takes the lead, then slows down to the original pace.
- As soon a O1 takes the lead, O2 does the same, followed eventually by all of the other players.
- Repeat until everyone has gone by the entire group a selected number of times.

OPTIONAL: Give a basketball to the last two players in line. After speed dribbling to the front of the formation, the ball is flipped over the head to the next person in line. The ball continues down the entire succession in this manner until the last person receives it. The trailing person now speed dribbles to the front of the line and continues as before.

16

BUDDY JUMPS

Primary Skill: Conditioning

Objective: To improve the vertical jump.

Equipment Needed: One stopwatch.

Coaching Tips to Players:
Maintain control and don't speed when first attempting this drill.

Procedure:

- Players will match up with someone of about the same size.

- O1 crouches down low to the floor.

- O2 stands beside O1. On the "Go" command, O2 begins rapidly jumping back and forth over O1 for twenty seconds.

- Players should jump from both feet and land on both feet.

- Players will switch positions after the allotted time.

- Execute three sets of 20 seconds each.

NOTE: Position of the lower player.

CAPITAL M

Primary Skill: Conditioning

Objective: To develop agility and balance.

Equipment Needed: None.

Coaching Tips to Players: Do not cross the feet when sliding.

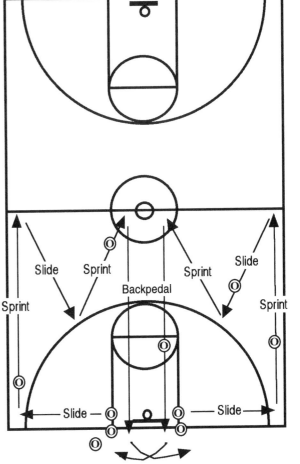

Procedure:

- Players form two lines under the basket and perform the following tasks, spelling out the letter "M":
  a. Defensive slide to the corner.
  b. Sprint to half court.
  c. Defensive slide to the three-point arc.
  d. Sprint to the jump circle.
  e. Backpedal to the baseline.
- Switch lines after each completed circuit.
- Each player runs a predetermined number of times.

NOTE: This is a great warm-up drill.

OPTIONAL: Change the drill pattern to spell out a "B", "D", "O", or "R". Be sure to mirror image it on the right side of the court.

FINGER SPINS

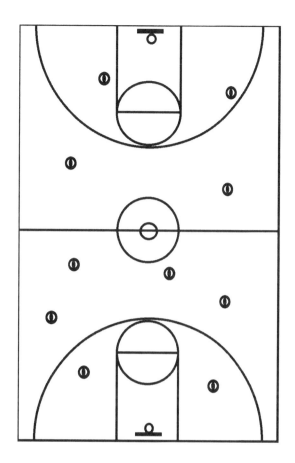

Primary Skill: Conditioning

Objective: To develop hand and eye coordination.

Equipment Needed: One ball for each player.

Coaching Tips to Players: The faster the ball spins the easier it is to balance.

Procedure:

- Each player grabs a ball, all players spread out around the floor.
- Participants practice the following stunts:
    a. Spin the ball on any finger for as long as possible.
    b. Spin the ball on any finger and use the free hand to keep it revolving.
    c. Transfer the ball from finger to finger while it is constantly in motion.
    d. Transfer the ball from one hand to the other hand while it is whirling.
    e. Spin the ball on the finger, push it slightly up into the air, punch it with a knuckle, then catch it back on the finger.
    f. Spin the ball on the finger, push it into the air, bump it with the forehead, then catch it on the finger again.
    g. Pair up and transfer a spinning ball to the partner.
    h. Simultaneously spin two balls.

FOLLOW THE LEADER

Primary Skill: Conditioning

Objective: To develop defensive conditioning and technique.

Equipment Needed: Stopwatch.

Coaching Tips to Players:
Athletes should push off with the foot each time.

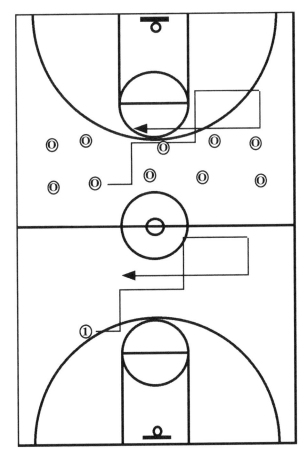

Procedure:

- All players spread out on the floor and assume a defensive stance.

- O1 faces the group and begins moving around the court as if playing defense.

- The entire group shadows O1's movements.

- All participants must make ninety-degree cuts during directional changes. (Do not round the corners.)

- Start the clock and run for three minutes.

- A different player comes to the front to lead the group every 30 seconds.

OPTIONAL: Every other day, add one minute to the original start time. Work toward a goal of ten minutes without stopping.

OPTIONAL: Each time the whistle is blown, all the players drop and perform a given number of push-ups, sit-ups, or whatever the coach commands. Upon completion, they spring back up and continue to follow the leader.

GLIDERS

Primary Skill: Conditioning

Objective: To develop cardiovascular endurance.

Equipment Needed: None.

Coaching Tips to Players:
Work hard the first half of the journey.

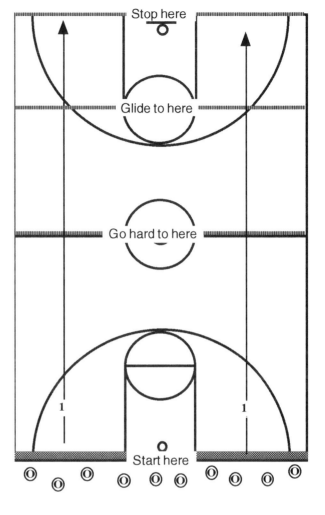

Procedure:

- All players line up on the end line.
- They go hard to half court, glide to the far foul line, and stop at the other end.
- Repeat the same moves coming back.
- This is not a race.
- Players will perform various actions to half court such as:
  - a. Sprint.
  - b. Hop off both legs like a frog.
  - c. Run backwards.
  - d. Alternate three hops with each leg.
  - e. Skip.
  - f. Side slide.
  - g. Zig Zag.

HOUR GLASS

Primary Skill: Conditioning

Objective: To enhance cardiovascular endurance.

Equipment Needed: One stopwatch.

Coaching Tips to Players: When side sliding, never cross the feet.

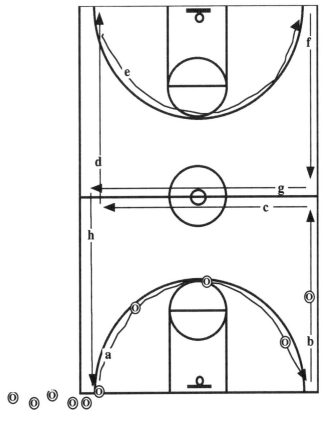

Procedure:

- The entire team lines up at the end of the court. One player is the leader.
- Participants always face the far end of the court.
- While traveling in an hour-glass pattern, athletes perform the following:
  a. Right curved defensive slide.
  b. Sprint forward.
  c. Left lateral defensive slide.
  d. Sprint forward.
  e. Right curved defensive slide.
  f. Backpedal.
  g. Left lateral defensive slide.
  h. Backpedal.
- Continue for a set amount of time or completed number of circuits.

JUMP ROPES

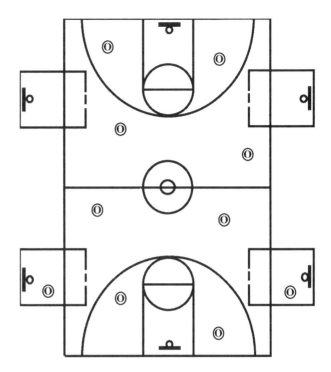

Primary Skill: Conditioning

Objective: To develop cardio-vascular endurance.

Equipment Needed: One jump rope for each player.

Coaching Tips to Players: Stay focused about not missing.

Procedure:

- Each player gets a jump rope.
- Players spread out to allow plenty of room between them and then do as follows:
    a. Jump rope a selected number of minutes in one place.
    b. Jump rope a set amount of time while moving around the court.
    c. Jump rope a set number of times without an error.
- Players will demonstrate several variations such as:
    a. Jumping while the rope is spinning backward.
    b. Jumping on one leg.
    c. Alternating legs each jump.
    d. Creating a routine that includes several styles.

OPTIONAL: Attempt to set a team or personal record of how many jumps can be completed in one minute without a miss.

LIFTS – ANKLES

Primary Skill: Conditioning

Objective: To increase the vertical jump.

Equipment Needed: None.

Coaching Tips to Players: Extend through the full range of motion.

Procedure:

- Players pair up and spread out around the floor.
- The rear person places both hands on the shoulders of the front individual and exerts moderate downward pressure.
- The front person raises up as high as possible on the toes and then back down.
- Repeat this twenty-five times.
- Switch positions. Each individual performs two sets of twenty-five.

A.   B.

24

LIFTS – JUMP AND REACH

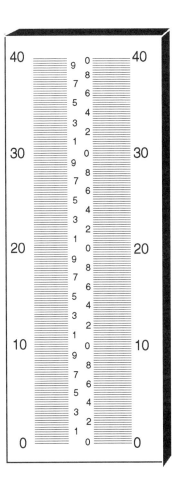

Primary Skill: Conditioning

Objective: To increase vertical jump.

Equipment Needed: The vertical jump board may have to be made. A 70-inch scale works well. This board is fixed to the wall and should begin about five feet up from the floor.

Coaching Tips to Players: Use the arms and explode upwards.

NOTE: Continue this scale up to 70 inches. ⟶

Procedure:

- Tell players to do the following:
  - a. Reach up and touch the board. Remember this initial mark.
  - b. Now, jump up as high as possible and touch the board again. Do this three times. Record the highest mark of the three jumps. Subtract the initial mark from the highest mark to determine the vertical jump.
- Two to three times each week, have the players record their vertical jump. Check for improvement over the season.

EXAMPLE: The initial mark is 13 and the highest mark is 37. The vertical jump reach is equal to 37 - 13 or 24 inches.

OPTIONAL: Use a chalkboard mounted to the wall, chalk, and a yardstick to measure the distance between the highest mark and the start mark.

OPTIONAL: Record and post the improvements of each player. Add them together and determine the total team improvement. Post the improvement weekly.

LIFTS – QUADS

Primary Skill: Conditioning

Objective: To increase the vertical jump.

Equipment Needed: None.

Coaching Tips to Players:
Explode with each lift.

Procedure:

- Players pair up and disperse around the court.
- The back person places both hands on the shoulders of the front person and pulls down with moderate force.
- The front player does a one-third squat, then explodes back to the standing position.
- The heels do **not** leave the floor.
- Repeat this movement 15 times.
- Swap assignments and repeat. Each player does two sets of 15.

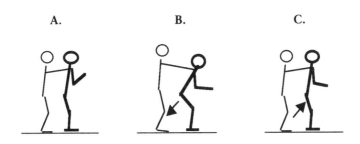

A.   B.   C.

LINE HOPS

Primary Skill: Conditioning

Objective: To enhance foot speed and body balance.

Equipment Needed: Stopwatch, floor tape, or painted lines already on the floor.

Coaching Tips to Players: Set a goal of how many times a movement will take place in the allotted time.

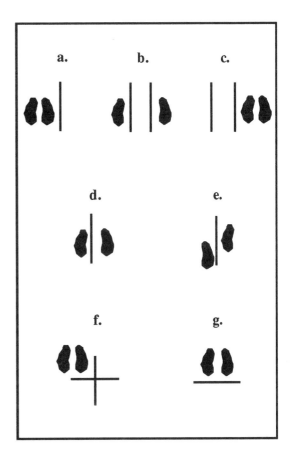

Procedure:

- Use various lines on the floor or tape some down.
- Players will jump as fast as possible for 10 seconds at each station listed below:
  a. Side hop - Jump sideways back and forth over a single line.
  b. Heel click - Jump and click heels together.
  c. Side hop - Same as "a" except the lines are 18 to 24 inches apart.
  d. Spinners - Jump and face in the opposite direction. Jump to the right and then back to the left.
  e. Cross step - Start with the legs crossed. Jump and cross them to the opposite sides.
  f. Four square - Jump into each square.
  g. Bunny hops - Jump forward and backward.

LINERS

Primary Skill: Conditioning

Objective: To develop cardio-vascular endurance.

Equipment Needed: None.

Coaching Tips to Players:
Push off hard when changing directions.

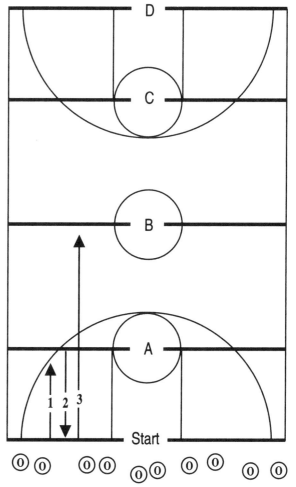

Procedure:

- All players line up on the end line.
- Each one performs the following:
    a. Sprint to line "A" and back to "start".
    b. Sprint to line "B" and return to "start".
    c. Dash to line "C" and back to "start".
    d. Run to line "D" and back to "start".

OPTIONAL: Players must run backwards when returning to the start line.

OPTIONAL: Pair up and alternate the liners.

OPTIONAL: Change the step pattern each time there is a forward directional change. For an example, these could be to jog, hop, skip, or defensive side slide.

OPTIONAL: Record the number of liners in a given amount of time.

OPTIONAL: Create three teams and have a relay race.

OCTOPUS

Primary Skill: Conditioning

Objective: To enhance cardiovascular endurance.

Equipment Needed: None.

Coaching Tips to Players:
Change your pace and directions
often.

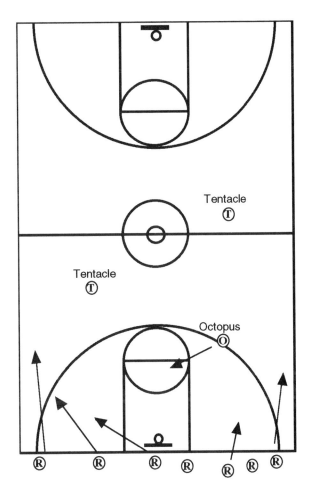

Procedure:

- Use a basketball court for the boundaries.

- O1 is the **octopus** and will start the runners by yelling "Octopus". Runners are no longer safe behind the end line. O1 will chase and seek to tag the runners.

- Runners line up on one end. On the command from the octopus, the runners attempt to travel to the other end line without going out of bounds or being tagged.

- Tagged runners will sit down and become **tentacles**. If a tentacle touches a passing runner, that runner must sit down too.

- Repeat this process until there are only one or two players remaining.

NOTE: Be sure the safe areas have enough room so that runners do not crash into the wall. Use the keys as a safe zone if there is not enough room at the ends of the court.

OPTIONAL: Designate two players to be an octopus.

OPTIONAL: Narrow the width of the court.

ONE-ON-ONE HALF COURT

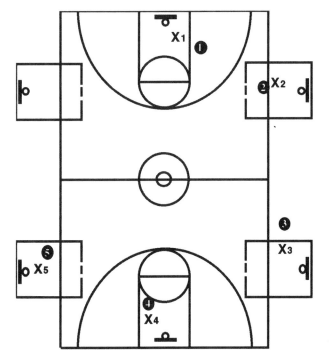

Primary Skill: Conditioning

Objective: To develop cardio-vascular endurance.

Equipment Needed: One basketball for each pair.

Coaching Tips to Players: Concentrate at all times.

© 1999 by Parker Publishing Company

Procedure:

- Develop a round robin or double elimination tournament bracket. (See the section on tournaments for forms and instructions.)
- All of the rules of basketball apply.
- The ball must be brought out beyond the foul line extended on any exchange of possession except on any turnover, steal, or shot that does not hit the rim or backboard.
- First player to score a set number of points is the winner.
- The offensive player will call fouls.
- Top three finishers of the tournament will receive some type of reward.

OPTIONAL: When a player makes the shot, he or she retains possession.

OPTIONAL: Play each game for a predetermined number of minutes. The player who is ahead after time expires is declared the winner.

PEDAL PUSHERS

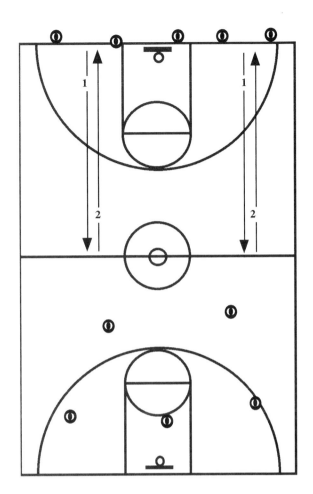

Primary Skill: Conditioning

Objective: To develop hand and eye coordination.

Equipment Needed: One ball for each player.

Coaching Tips to Players: Maintain relaxed hands.

Diagram Notes: Upper court illustrates the drill options that require movement to half court and back.

Procedure:

- Players spread out along the end line.
- Each player bends over at the waist and remains in one location.
- Everyone begins shuffling their feet forward and backward.
- They next start passing the ball back and forth (in a figure eight pattern) **behind** the front leg with each foot exchange.
- Once the stationary method has been attempted, have each player walk to half court and back while doing the figure-eight pattern.

OPTIONAL: Have the players sprint to half court and back.

OPTIONAL: Have relay races to half court and back.

OPTIONAL: Count how many times an individual can shuffle the ball back and forth in one minute. Over and back is considered one time.

OPTIONAL: Time how fast they can travel to half court and back.

PENDULUM

Primary Skill: Conditioning

Objective: To develop hand reflex speed and timing.

Equipment Needed: One ball for each player.

Coaching Tips to Players: Concentrate.

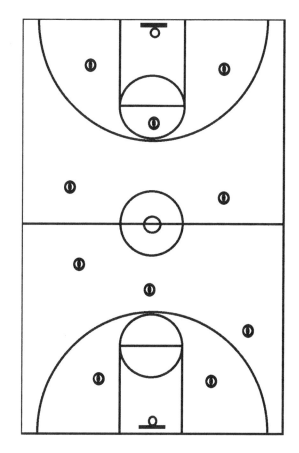

Procedure:

• Pass the ball back and forth between the legs.

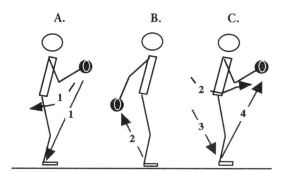

OPTIONAL: How many times can the ball be passed back and forth in a given time?

OPTIONAL: How hard can the ball be slammed to the floor and still be caught on the back or front side?

32

PERFECT WEAVE

Primary Skill: Conditioning

Objective: To develop teamwork and ball control.

Equipment Needed: Two basketballs.

Coaching Tips to Players: Stay focused and alert.

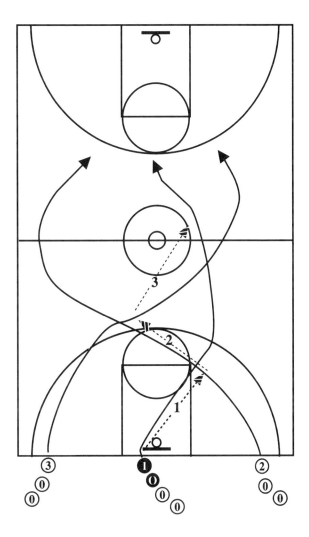

Procedure:

- Players divide into three lines.
- Start the drill at one end of the basketball court.
- The ball starts in the middle line.
- The passer will always travel **behind** the person who received the ball.
- O1 passes the ball to O2, then scampers behind O2.
- O2 receives the ball from O1, passes it to O3, then dashes behind O3.
- O3 receives the ball from O2, passes it to O1, and the routine is repeated to the other end of the court. Upon arriving, a player shoots a lay-in. The threesome regroups, returns to the near end using the same three-person weave, and shoots a second lay-in.
- If either lay-in is missed, then that group must repeat the weave over and over until both lay-ins are made.

OPTIONAL: The team must make a predetermined number of lay-ins in a row.

POPCORN

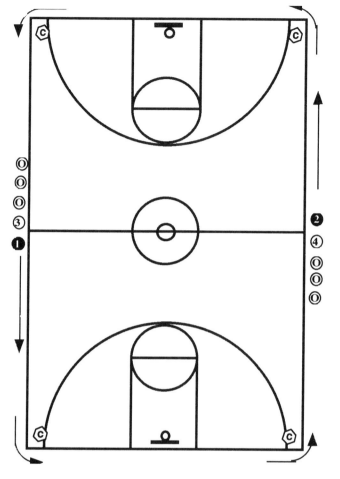

Primary Skill: Conditioning

Objective: To develop team-work and endurance.

Equipment Needed: Two basketballs and four floor cones.

Coaching Tips to Players: Keep the feet moving, even when waiting to catch the ball.

Procedure:

- Split the team in half.
- Each half will line up behind a basketball on opposite sides near half court.
- This drill is continuous.
- O1 and O2, who are on opposite sides of the court, start by simultaneously throwing their ball straight up into the air and running around the cones to the other side.
- O3 and O4 step forward, catch the ball, toss it straight up, and sprint off.
- The next player in each line catches the ball and models the previous individual.
- The ball should remain at half court and not be allowed to touch the floor for two minutes.

OPTIONAL: Administer penalties, such as sit-ups, when the ball does hit the floor.

OPTIONAL: Restart the time each time the ball hits the floor.

OPTIONAL: Place a ball at each corner, make four groups, and do likewise.

RELAY – JUMP SHOT

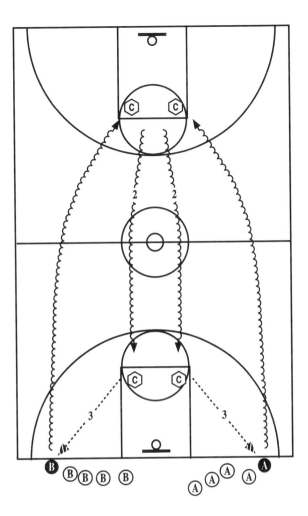

Primary Skill: Conditioning

Objective: To develop endurance and the competitive spirit.

Equipment Needed: Two basketballs and four cones.

Coaching Tips to Players: Stay focused.

Procedure:

- Players form two equal teams.
- When teams are uneven, have one player go twice.
- Players gather at opposite corners on the same end of a court.
- The first players in each line dribble as fast as possible to the far cone, stop, and have three attempts to make a jump shot. All missed shots must be rebounded and launched again from behind the cone. After any made shot or a missed third try, the ball is rebounded, and dribbled to the opposite end. The player has three more chances to make a jump shot.
- After completing the circuit, the ball is passed to the next person in line and play continues.
- To determine a winner, have each player go down and back twice.

OPTIONAL: Move the cones to different locations.

RELAY – PARTNER TAG

Primary Skill: Conditioning

Objective: To develop cardiovascular endurance.

Equipment Needed: One timing device.

Coaching Tips to Players: Focus on the task at hand.

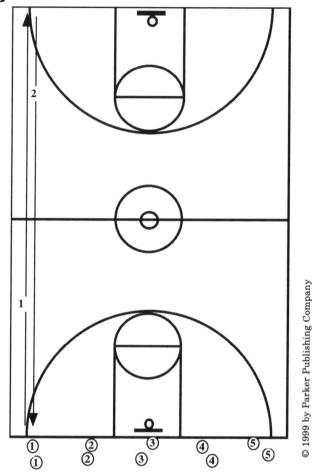

Procedure:

- Each player picks a partner and lines up at the end line.
- Teams will race against the clock for one minute.
- The objective is to sprint down and back a predetermined number of times. Down and back is one trek.
- Alternate travel between the partners.
- The next runner may begin when the partner's hand is tagged.

EXAMPLE: A goal for college men could be 8 trips. For high school boys, it could be 7-1/2 excursions.

OPTIONAL: Change the sprint distance to half court and back.

OPTIONAL: Place three individuals on a team. Challenge the other teams to a race.

OPTIONAL: Each time the drill is used, players must choose a different partner.

RELAY – SPEED DRIBBLE

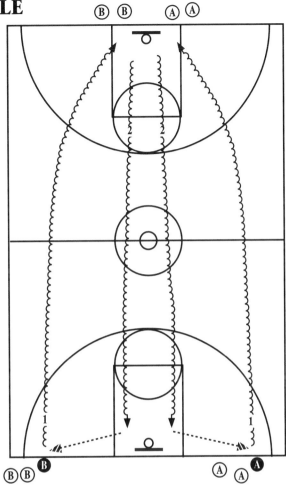

Primary Skill: Conditioning

Objective: To develop endurance and the competitive spirit.

Equipment Needed: One basketball for each team.

Coaching Tips to Players: Keep the ball below the waist to maintain control.

Procedure:

- Players form two equal teams. If they are unequal, then one player must go twice.

- Players gather at opposite sides on both end lines. (See the above diagram.)

- The first player in line will dribble as fast as possible to the other end and make the lay-in. If the shot is missed, the shooter must stay until the basket is made. After the shot is made, the ball is passed to a teammate at the opposite end and the race is continued.

- The first team to make a predetermined number of lay-ins is declared the winner.

- Teams should switch sides after a winner has been determined and race again.

NOTE: Because of two way traffic, keep the first lines wide and the return lines centered.

OPTIONAL: Change the type of shot.

OPTIONAL: Teams are required to make a predetermined number in a row. When there is a miss, that team must start over.

RUNNING SNAKE

Primary Skill: Conditioning

Objective: To develop agility and foot speed.

Equipment Needed: None.

Coaching Tips to Players:
Push off with the outside foot to accelerate directional change.

Procedure:

- All players spread out in a line.
- Establish 5 to 6 feet of space between each player in line.
- Players should not bump, touch, or graze any of the other players standing in line.
- O1 zips back and forth through the line until reaching the other end. Once there, O1 creates a 5 to 6 foot buffer and stays put.
- O2 begins to pursue O1 when O1 is approximately three players ahead.
- O3 gives chase when O2 is about three players in front.
- All other players copy the previous action so that the drill becomes continuous.
- The snake may meander anywhere on the court.
- Continue until everyone has zig zagged through the line five times.

OPTIONAL: Try to tag the player in front.

OPTIONAL: Players must stop and change direction on every sound of the whistle.

SHUTTLE RUN

Primary Skill: Conditioning

Objective: To increase quickness, speed, and agility.

Equipment Needed: One stopwatch and four erasers or pick up items.

Coaching Tips to Players: Stay low and push off hard.

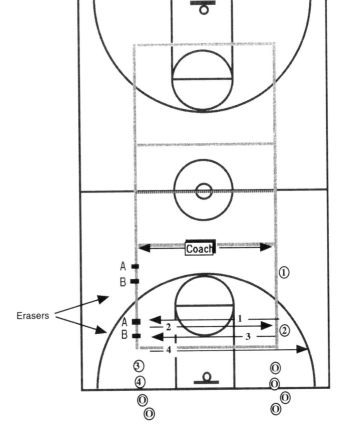

Erasers

Procedure:

- Place four erasers 30 feet apart. This is the width of a volleyball court.

- Make two lines of participants. This speeds up the event because the runners do not have to return the erasers after each race.

- O1 and O2 begin on the "Go" command from the coach. They will sprint down, pick up eraser "A", turn, sprint back to the start/finish line, **set** the eraser on the line, turn, sprint back and pick up eraser "B", turn, and sprint past the start/finish line.

- The coach will announce times, proceed to the other end, and initiate the next race between O3 and O4.

- Allow two races for each contestant.

OPTIONAL: Each athlete will set a goal to improve upon the first time by no less than half a second during the season.

OPTIONAL: Post the improvements.

THIEVES

Primary Skill: Conditioning

Objective: To develop foot speed and endurance.

Equipment Needed: Five hula hoops and 12 to 16 basketballs.

Coaching Tips to Players: Push off hard during the stop and go.

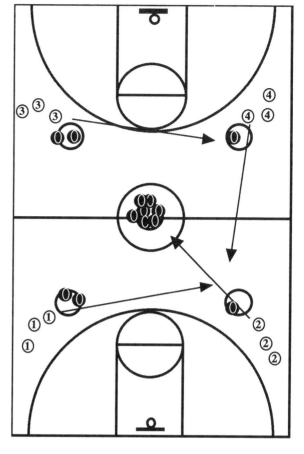

Procedure:

- Four teams line up behind a hula hoop. Put all of the balls in the center hoop.
- On the command "Go", the first person in each line will sprint to the middle, retrieve one ball, dribble back to their hoop, set the ball down, and go to the end of the line.
- The next player may go as soon as the ball has been set down inside the hoop.
- Only one runner from each team is allowed in the theater of play.
- After the first thieves have taken a ball from the middle hoop, the next runners may go to any hula hoop, remove one ball, and return it to their own cache.
- When a team has collected a predetermined number, they are the winners.

OPTIONAL: Start with the balls in each of the four corners and be first to have zero. Do not use the center hoop.

OPTIONAL: After a time limit, the team in possession of the most basketballs wins.

OPTIONAL: Begin each new game with one less basketball in the middle.

TIME LAPSE

Primary Skill: Conditioning

Objective: To improve cardio-vascular endurance.

Equipment Needed: One stopwatch and four cones.

Coaching Tips to Players: Set and maintain a pace.

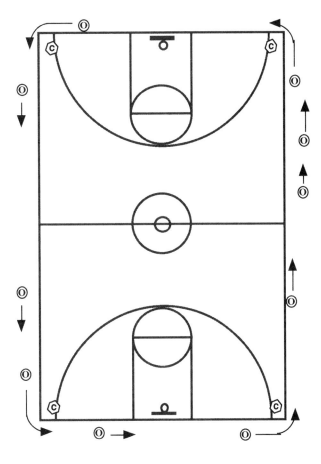

Procedure:

- The entire team spreads out around the perimeter of the court.
- Players run around the outside of the court for a total of 15 minutes.
- The athletes will run:
  a. five minutes clockwise,
  b. four minutes counter clockwise,
  c. followed by three minutes clockwise,
  d. two minutes counter clockwise, and
  e. finally finish one minute clockwise.

OPTIONAL: Have the participants start out at a jog and with each direction change, pick up the pace so that the last minute is a sprint.

OPTIONAL: Pair up the athletes. One player runs while the other jogs. When the runner comes back around and tags their partner, their roles are reversed.

TIP-N-SPRINT

Primary Skill: Conditioning

Objective: To develop teamwork, ball control, and cardiovascular endurance.

Equipment Needed: Two basketballs.

Coaching Tips to Players: Jump up and meet the ball.

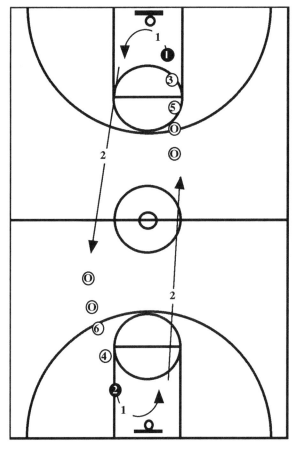

Procedure:

- Players divide into two units with one unit at each end of the court.
- O1 and O2 tip the ball against the backboard simultaneously and sprint to the opposite end.
- O3 follows and mimics O1.
- O4 follows and apes O2.
- Play is continuous.
- Do not let the ball touch the floor.
- Execute the drill for a predetermined amount of time.

OPTIONAL: If the task at hand is to difficult for youngsters, have them jump up, catch the ball, come down with it, then jump back up, and shoot or toss it against the backboard.

OPTIONAL: When a ball touches the floor, the time is started over.

TWELVE-MINUTE RUN

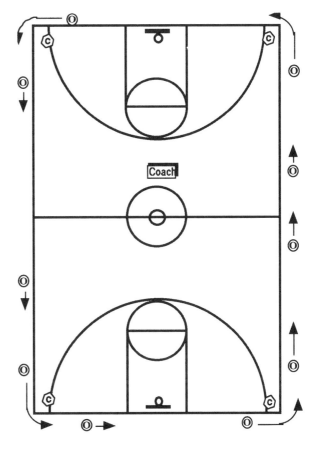

Primary Skill: Conditioning

Objective: To build and enhance cardiovascular endurance.

Equipment Needed: One stopwatch and four floor cones.

Coaching Tips to Players:
Attempt to pass someone during the last two or three laps.

Procedure:

- Players line up around the outside of a basketball court.

- All participants continually run around the floor for 12 minutes.

- Do not cut inside of the floor cones.

- Participants should keep track of the number of laps completed and try to improve the next time.

NOTE: Eighteen laps around a 84′ × 50′ basketball court is approximately one mile.

OPTIONAL: Post a chart on the wall and record individual results and improvements.

OPTIONAL: Pair up the athletes. One player runs while the other jogs. When the runner comes back around and tags their partner, the roles are reversed.

OPTIONAL: Pair up the athletes. One partner runs clockwise on the inside of the out of bounds line while the other runs counter clockwise on the outside. Record how many times the pair can pass each other while traveling in opposite directions for 12 minutes.

UP AND DOWN

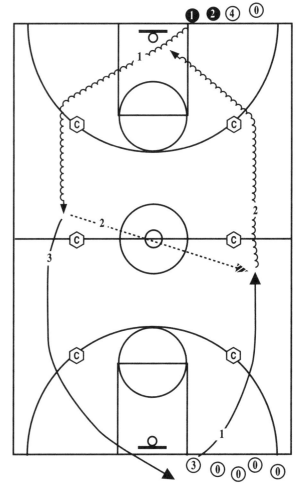

Primary Skill: Conditioning

Objective: To increase shooting and passing accuracy under fatigue.

Equipment Needed: Two basketballs and six cones.

Coaching Tips to Players: Concentrate.

Procedure:

- Players form two lines on opposite ends of the basketball court.
- Action is continuous.
- O1 and O2 possess a ball.
- O1 begins by dribbling outside the first two cones, then passes the ball to O3 near half court. Both players are on the move. O1 goes to the end of the far line.
- O3 leaves when O1 dribbles beyond the first cone. Staying outside the cones, O3 receives the pass from O1, dribbles on down and shoots a lay-in.
- O2 takes off as soon as O1 has passed the ball to O3.
- O4 grabs the rebound from the lay-in and follows O2 after O2 passes the ball.
- Switch sides after a set amount of time so that the left side lay-ins are also practiced.

OPTIONAL: Move the cones five feet closer together. Each set of players must pass the ball back and forth three times while moving down the court.

WALL JUMPS

Primary Skill: Conditioning

Objective: To improve the vertical jump.

Equipment Needed: A wall.

Coaching Tips to Players: Explode each jump.

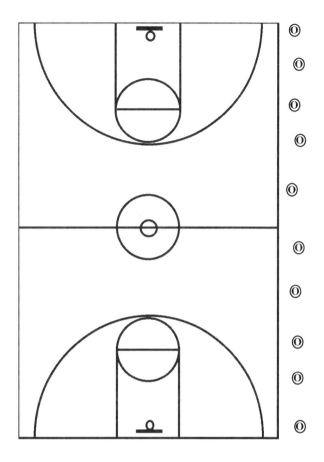

Procedure:

- Players line up against the wall.
- Players will jump as high as possible each time.
- They will jump 10 times in a row using the
    a. right hand,
    b. left hand,
    c. both hands, and
    d. alternate hands.

OPTIONAL: Players will jump up and touch the net or rim, sprint to and touch the free throw line, then return and touch the net. Repeat a predetermined number of times. Change the use of hands as above.

OPTIONAL: Pair up and face a partner. The hands are constantly held high above the head. Alternate jumping so that teammates are not touching the floor at the same time.

WHISTLE REVERSES

Primary Skill: Conditioning

Objective: To develop cardiovascular endurance and the ability to change directions quickly.

Equipment Needed: One whistle.

Coaching Tips to Players:
Push off hard when beginning each direction change.

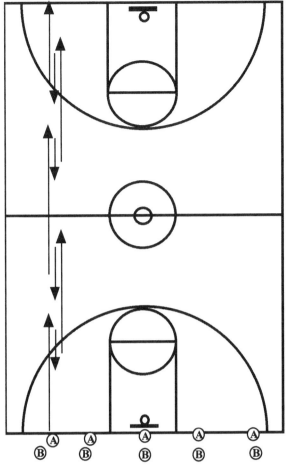

Procedure:

- Players divide into "A" and "B" groups and report to the end line.

- The coach blows the whistle and the entire "A" group begins sprinting forward. On the second whistle, they stop as fast as possible and run backwards until the third whistle. With each whistle there is a change of direction.

- Force five to eight directional changes before allowing anyone to reach the far end.

- Team "B" goes after group "A" has finished.

- Each unit will repeat the drill a selected number of times.

OPTIONAL: Players must alternate between sprinting and defensive sliding, with each new forward direction change.

OPTIONAL: Each time there is a forward whistle, participants must drop and do five set ups, five jumping jacks, or five push ups.

Section 4

DEFENSE

It's not the size of the dog in the fight,
it's the size of the fight in the dog.

—Mark Twain

BLOCK THAT POINT

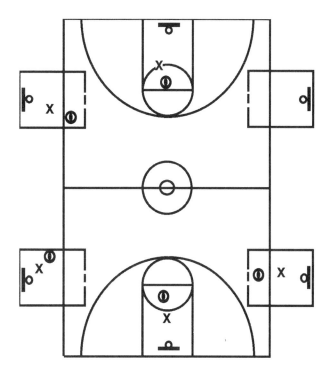

Primary Skill: Defense

Objective: To develop the potential for blocking the shot.

Equipment Needed: One basketball and one baseball glove for each pair of players.

Coaching Tips to Players: Jump straight up when attempting the block.

Procedure:

- Players pair up with a teammate of about equal ability or size.

- Pairs compete in a game of basketball within the boundaries of the key.

- If there are not enough keys available, one pair should share with another pair.

- The defender wears a baseball glove and tries to block, deflect, or alter the shot.

- Each person has five consecutive chances to score.

- Each shot counts as one chance, whether the basket is made or missed.

- Alternate until each player has had 15 shot attempts.

- A field goal is worth two points and a foul shot is worth one.

- Fouls will constitute one chance at a free throw shot and repossession of the ball.

- Free throws will not count as one of the five attempts.

OPTIONAL: Put a baseball glove on each hand.

OPTIONAL: Take the glove off and play a regulation game of basketball in the same space.

CHAIR SLIDE

Primary Skill: Defense

Objective: To develop proper defensive posture.

Equipment Needed: Two chairs for each player.

Coaching Tips to Players: Do not cross the feet.

Procedure:

- Place two chairs about 15 feet apart.
- A player sits in a chair, raises up about three inches, defensive slides to the second chair, and sits down by dropping approximately three inches.
- This should be practiced eight to ten times.
- Then players play musical chairs. Have one less chair than the total number of players involved. The defensive slide technique must be used at all times. Remove one chair each time the whistle is blown. Eliminated players will run a predetermined number of line sprints.
- Arrange the chairs in a circle or in two rows with the backs of the chairs touching or possibly two rows facing in the same direction.

OPTIONAL: A quick double whistle will cause a directional change.

OPTIONAL: Use music. When it stops, all must sit.

DEFIANT "D"

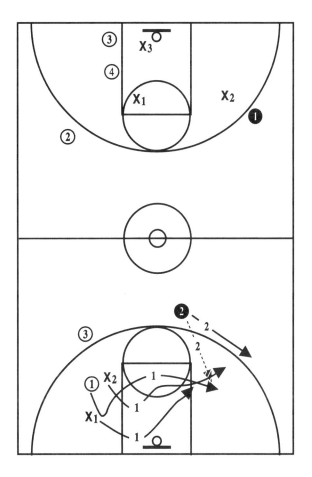

Primary Skill: Defense

Objective: To prevent the ball from getting inside.

Equipment Needed: One basketball for each group.

Coaching Tips to Players: Attempt to keep an arm in the passing lane.

Diagram Notes: The upper court illustrates the drill with two extra players for more challenge.

Procedure:

- Players break into groups of five. Three in each group are on offense, and two on defense.

- O1 moves around inside the three point arc, attempting to get open for a pass. O1 may not dribble the ball and will pass it back to either O2 or O3.

- O2 and O3 are above the three point arc and may shift around at will. They are not allowed to dribble though. They may only pass to each other once before having to pass the ball inside to O1. Scoring is not allowed.

- The offense may not hold the ball for more than five seconds.

- The two defenders will attempt to prevent the ball from getting in or out.

- Rotate after the defense creates a given number of turnovers, steals, deflections, or the offense has passed the ball a given number of times.

OPTIONAL: Allow O1, O2, O3, and O4 to score against X1, X2, and X3.

DOUBLE VISION

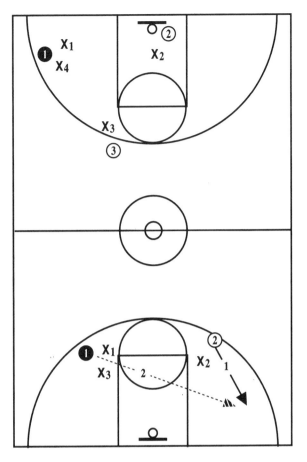

Primary Skill: Defense

Objective: To put extreme pressure on the ball.

Equipment Needed: One basketball.

Coaching Tips to Players: Quickly stop the dribble.

Diagram Notes: The upper court illustrates the drill with two extra players for more challenge.

Procedure:

- Players break into groups of five.
- Form teams with the defense getting one extra player.
- The games are played in a half-court area.
- Keep a double team on the ball at all times.
- The object is to be the first team to score six points.
- All four teams are competing to get six points first even though two separate games are being played at the same time.
- The offense receives two points each time they score a basket.
- The defense receives two points each time they prevent the offense from scoring.
- After a given number of turnovers, a predetermined score, or an allotted amount of time, allow the players to mix and match teammates, and begin a new contest.

OPTIONAL: Authorize O1, O2, and O3 to challenge four defensive players.

DOWN THE TUBE

Primary Skill: Defense

Objective: To recover and intercept a pass after the ball has passed by.

Equipment Needed: One basketball for each group.

Coaching Tips to Players: Do not be afraid to anticipate and gamble on the pass.

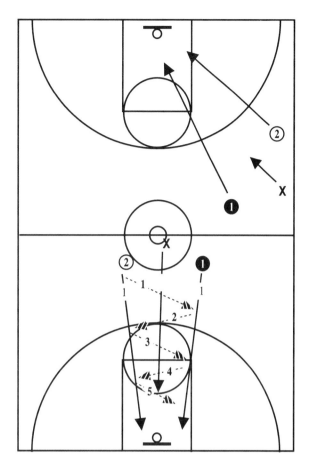

Procedure:

- Players form three lines.

- Dribbling is not allowed.

- O1 and O2 must pass the ball to each other four times while trying to score.

- The defender starts six feet behind O1 and O2. As soon as O1 passes the ball to O2, the defender takes chase and attempts to deflect or intercept the ball.

- Switch lines each time.

OPTIONAL: Form three lines at one end and use the full court.

OPTIONAL: When using the full court, if the defender is successful, they will immediately speed dribble to the other end and attempt to score. O1 and O2 will now give chase.

OPTIONAL: When using the full court, if the defender is successful, they, along with the player who did not throw the errant pass, will join up and continue the drill to the other end. The player who threw the bad pass will then pursue.

FLASH PASS

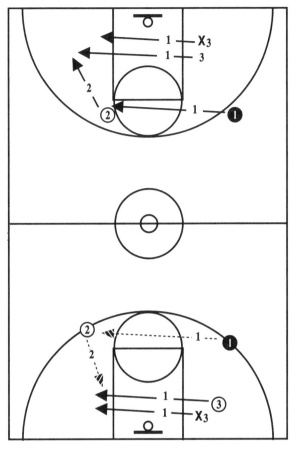

Primary Skill: Defense

Objective: To deny the low post pass.

Equipment Needed: One basketball per group of four.

Coaching Tips to Players: Move quickly to the spot.

Diagram Notes: The upper court illustrates the drill practiced from the opposite side of the court.

Procedure:

- Split the team in half.
- Use half of a basketball court.
- O1 tries to pass the ball to O3. If not, then O1 passes to O2.
- If O2 receives the first pass, then an honest attempt to pass the ball to O3 should take place. If this is not possible, then O2 passes the ball back to O1.
- O3 flashes from side to side trying to receive the pass from either O1 or O2. O3 may not shoot the ball, but instead will pass back to O1 or O2.
- The defensive player will try to prevent all passes to O3 by constantly playing arduous in-your-face "D".
- Switch positions after a predetermined number of attempts.

OPTIONAL: Allow O3 to score after a predetermined number of possessions.

OPTIONAL: Add an additional defensive player.

FORWARD DENIAL

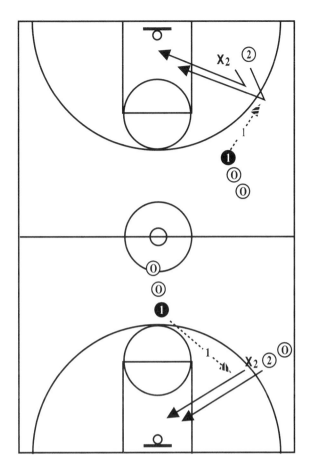

Primary Skill: Defense

Objective: To develop defensive pressure on all wing passes.

Equipment Needed: One basketball for each group of three players.

Coaching Tips to Players: The defender should attempt to put a hand into the passing lane.

Procedure:

- Divide the team in half.
- Use half of a basketball court.
- O1 attempts to pass to O2 but must stay in the same general area.
- O2 tries to get free for a pass from O1 but is not allowed to go back door the first five seconds. O2 is not allowed to score and must pass the ball back to O1 or O2 after each possession.
- The defensive player tries to prevent the pass to O2.
- Rotate positions after five denial attempts.
- Relocate to the other side of the floor after everyone has been on defense a given number of times.

OPTIONAL: Allow O3 to score after a predetermined number of possessions.

OPTIONAL: Add a defender against O1.

FOX AND HARE

Primary Skill: Defense and offense

Objective: To prevent the opponent from scoring.

Equipment Needed: One ball for each group and two floor cones.

Coaching Tips to Players: They that hesitate are lost.

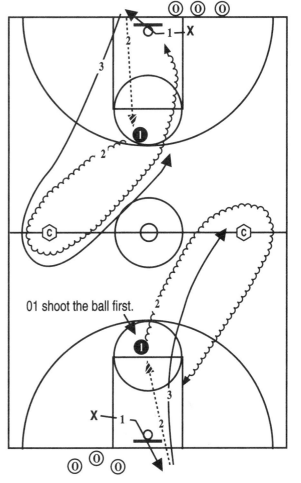

01 shoot the ball first.

Procedure:

- Players form two groups.
- Each group will locate a cone at half court.
- Use half of a basketball court for all of the action.
- O1 shoots a shot from inside the upper half of the circle. While remaining in the circle, O1 receives the ball back from the defender, dribbles around the cone at half court, then returns to score a lay in.
- The defender gets the rebound, made or missed, steps out of bounds and passes the ball to O1. Next the defender gives chase and must follow O1 in the same direction around the cone. The defender attempts to prevent O1 from scoring.
- Switch positions each time.

OPTIONAL: Use the full court so that the offensive person is required to dribble to the opposite end to score.

GO GET IT

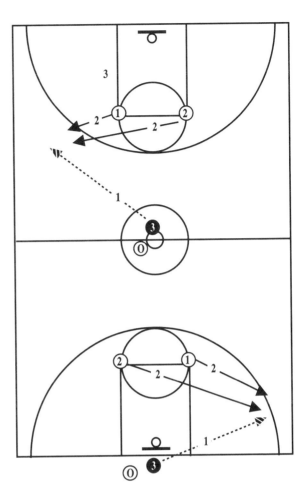

Primary Skill: Defense

Objective: To develop aggressive defensive demeanor.

Equipment Needed: One basketball for each group of three or four players.

Coaching Tips to Players: Be aggressive but maintain body control.

Diagram Notes: The upper court illustrates the drill with the ball being put into play from the center of the court.

Procedure:

- Players form groups of four or five.
- Play is at half court.
- O1 and O2 go to the foul line, face down court, and remain motionless. At the command of "Go," both O1 and O2 go after the ball. The player who gains possession of the ball has ten seconds in which to score. The other player attempts to deny the score.
- Only one shot attempt is allowed, as in "Do or Die".
- O3 will slowly roll the ball in any direction.
- All players rotate after each attempt.

OPTIONAL: Start the contest with the ball being put into play from center court.

OPTIONAL: Allow the action to continue when the offensive player obtains the rebound.

OPTIONAL: O3 may enter the game after a five second countdown.

IN YOUR FACE

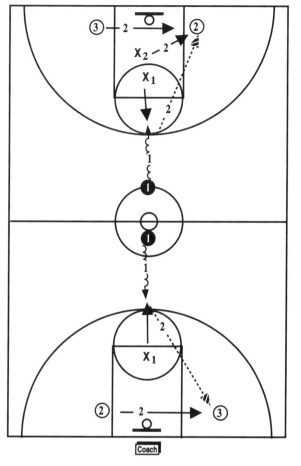

Primary Skill: Defense

Objective: To put intense pressure on the ball.

Equipment Needed: One basketball for each group.

Coaching Tips to Players: Force the offense into difficult passes and shots.

Diagram Notes: The upper court illustrates the drill with an additional defender for more confrontation.

Procedure:

- Players form groups of four or five.
- Use a half-court location.
- O1 dribbles to the top half of the free throw circle, pulls up, and waits for the coach to point to either O2 or O3. O1 now passes the ball to the selected player.
- The X1 starts at the free throw line, forces O1 to give up the dribble in the top half of the circle, then attempts to steal the ball or deflect the pass.
- If O2 receives the pass from O1, then O3 sprints across the lane to play defense.
- A player has only five seconds in which to score.
- Rotate positions each play.

OPTIONAL: O1 can choose where to pass.

OPTIONAL: Allow X1 to drop into the key and play defense.

OPTIONAL: Allow O1 to join in on offense.

LAWMAKER

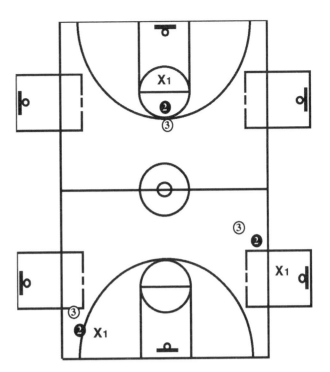

Primary Skill: Defense

Objective: To develop quick transitions from defense to offense.

Equipment Needed: One basketball for each group.

Coaching Tips to Players: Block out to ensure the rebound.

Diagram Notes: The floor illustrates play beginning from various locations.

Procedure:

- The team forms groups of three players behind the foul line at the various baskets.

- Everyone is against everyone else.

- Each must attempt to be the first person to score a predetermined number of points.

- X1 will attempt to prevent O2 from scoring. X1 will rebound the made or missed shot, become O1, **outlet** pass the ball to O3, and return to the end of the line behind O3.

- O2 will try to score against X1. O2 may rebound any missed shot or made basket, even out of the net, and score again. When O2 finally loses the ball, O2 will transform into X2 and attempt to prevent O3 from scoring. X2 may steal the outlet pass from O1 to O3 and score again against O1.

- O3 will receive the outlet from O1 and attempt to score against X2. Play is continuous.

OPTIONAL: Start play from a different location.

OPTIONAL: Allow only a predetermined number of dribbles or given amount of time.

MAKE IT COUNT

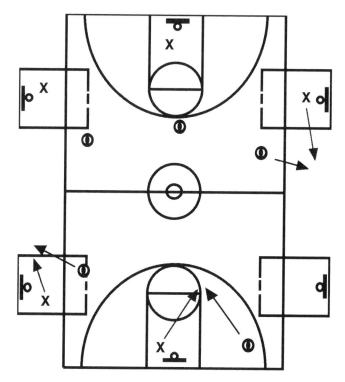

Primary Skill: Defense

Objective: To distract the shooter.

Equipment Needed: One ball for each pair of players.

Coaching Tips to Players: Make noise and arm movements.

© 1999 by Parker Publishing Company

Procedure:

- Each player pairs up with another player.

- Dribbling is not allowed for this drill.

- O1 may move around freely without the ball. When O1 makes the shot, then the defender fetches the ball and passes it back to O1. When the shot fails, O1 retrieves the rebound and passes it to the defender. The defender is now on offense with play continuing as before.

- The first player to reach a predetermined number of baskets is the winner.

- The looser will run a predetermined number of sprints.

OPTIONAL: Require players to shoot from a designated area each time.

OPTIONAL: Create a "Top Gun" or a round robin tournament. Keep individual records and reward the winner. See the information in the tournament section of this book on how to construct the brackets.

MISCHIEVOUS

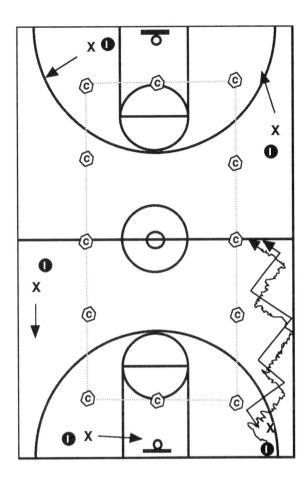

Primary Skill: Defense

Objective: To cause the dribbler to change directions or quit dribbling.

Equipment Needed: One ball for every two players plus 12 floor cones.

Coaching Tips to Players: Focus on the ball.

Procedure:

- Each player pairs up with a teammate.

- This drill is not designed to be a race.

- Players will slowly travel in the same direction around the course.

- O1 attempts to dribble past the defender within a ten foot wide lane. When O1 does get past the defender, O1 will slow up and let the defender reestablish position.

- The defender will guard the ball and not the person. The defense attempts to either steal the ball, force the dribbler to go out of bounds, cause a dribbling error, or make the dribbler stop dribbling. When successful, O1 will be allowed to regroup and continue.

- Positions will be switched after one completed lap.

- All players will reverse directions after a given time.

OPTIONAL: At the whistle, pairs will exchange roles and direction of travel.

NOMADS

Primary Skill: Defense

Objective: To develop proper spacing as the ball is moved around.

Equipment Needed: One basketball.

Coaching Tips to Players: Form triangles with the defender between the ball and the person being guarded.

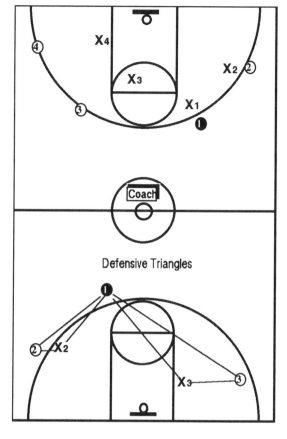

Defensive Triangles

Procedure:

- Players form groups of four defensive and four offensive players.
- Use half of the basketball court.
- The offense slowly passes the ball around the perimeter and allows the defenders to make proper adjustments.
- Each received pass must be held for a minimum of three seconds.
- The offense is not allowed to penetrate.
- The offense is not allowed to score.
- Switch roles after a predetermined amount of time.

OPTIONAL: Add a fifth player to each side.

OPTIONAL: Allow penetration and scoring.

OPTIONAL: Play a game to a predetermined number of points.

OPTIONAL: Use the full court to enhance conditioning.

PICKET "D" FENCE

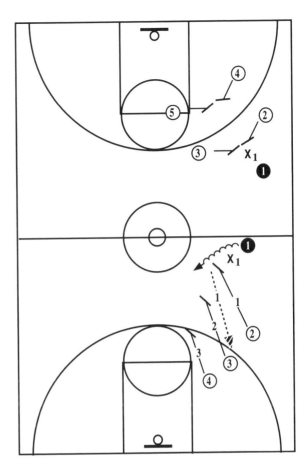

Primary Skill: Defense

Objective: To develop the ability to fight over multiple screens.

Equipment Needed: One ball for each line.

Coaching Tips to Players: Fight over the top of each screen.

Diagram Notes: Upper court illustrates the drill with the use of double screens.

Procedure:

- Players form groups of five or six players each.

- Each unit goes to opposite ends of the court.

- O1 starts with the ball and waits for O2's screen. O1 dribbles past this screen, stops, throws the ball to O3, waits for O3's return pass and screen, dribbles by it, stops, passes the ball to O4, waits for O4's return pass and screen, then concludes the process by attempting to score a lay-in. Only one shot attempt is allowed.

- X1 will fight hard to get by each screen. When X1 defeats the final screen, the immediate task is to stop the offensive player from scoring.

- O2, O3, and O4 will set sequential delayed screens against X1.

- Begin play from a variety of locations.

- Rotate positions frequently.

OPTIONAL: Set a series of double screens.

PREVENT

Primary Skill: Defense

Objective: To develop full court defensive pressure.

Equipment Needed: One ball for every two players plus six floor cones.

Coaching Tips to Players: Go slow at first.

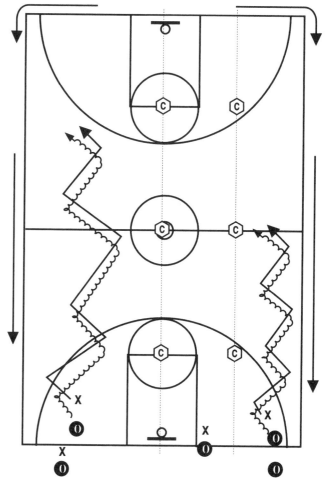

Procedure:

- Divide the court into half and then divide one of the halves again.

- All players pair up and go to one end of the court. Only two players are allowed in any lane at a time. They must stay in their own lanes during play.

- The offensive player attempts to dribble to the other end under control and works the defender back and forth.

- The defense attempts to either steal the ball, force the dribbler to go out of bounds, cause a dribbling error, or make the dribbler stop dribbling. If the defender causes any of the above, the offensive player retains the ball and resumes dribbling.

- Pairs should rotate lanes and change positions each time down.

OPTIONAL: The drill can be made continuous by having the players return back to the start line by going along the outside of the court.

SCREEN PICK

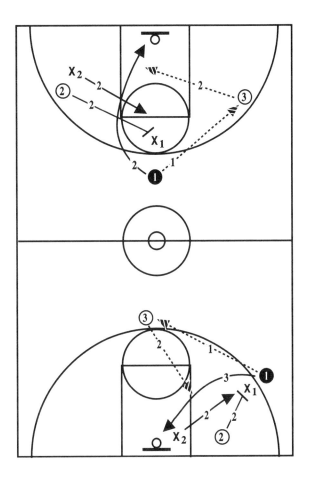

Primary Skill: Defense

Objective: To develop defensive skills for fighting around a screen.

Equipment Needed: One ball per group.

Coaching Tips to Players: Move quickly.

Diagram Notes: Upper court illustrates the drill with a screen set for the top offensive player.

© 1999 by Parker Publishing Company

Procedure:

- Players form groups of five.
- Use a half-court setting.
- O1 passes to O3, cuts past O2, looks for return pass from O3, and attempts to score a basket.
- O3 receives the pass from O1, then attempts to pass back to O1.
- O2 sets a screen against X1 as soon as O1 passes the ball.
- X1 endeavors to fight over or through the screen.
- X2 calls "Screen", then jumps out and into the path of O1 until X1 can recover.
- Offensive players should begin play from a variety of locations.
- Rotate positions frequently.

OPTIONAL: Add a defender against O2.

OPTIONAL: Add a fourth person to each side.

SHADOW

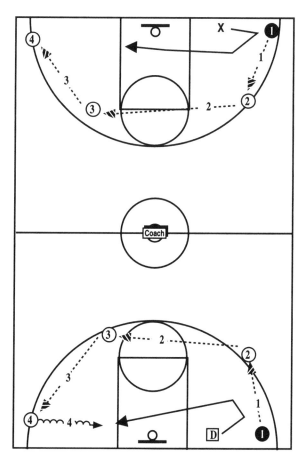

Primary Skill: Defense

Objective: To develop skills in a helping defense.

Equipment Needed: One ball per group.

Coaching Tips to Players: Attempt to watch both the ball and the offensive person.

Diagram Notes: Upper and lower court depicts the drill run from both sides.

Procedure:

- Players break into two groups and report to a half-court area.
- O1 receives the ball and has one attempt to drive the baseline. O1 next passes the ball to O2. O1 must stay in the same general area and now attempts to get open.
- If O2 can not pass the ball back to O1 in three seconds, O2 passes the ball to O3.
- If O3 can not pass the ball back to O1 in three seconds, O3 passes the ball to O4.
- O4 will wait for the coach to yell "now" and has three seconds in which to score.
- The defensive player will:
  a. Deny the baseline drive to O1.
  b. Deny the pass from all of the other players to O1.
  c. Attempt to stop O4 from scoring.
- Rotate one position clockwise after a player has been on defense.

SLIDE WAVE – TIGHT

Primary Skill: Defense

Objective: To develop defensive positioning while guarding the ball.

Equipment Needed: One ball for every two players.

Coaching Tips to Players: It is important that the offense works the defense so that skill development is maximized.

Procedure:

- Players pair up with a teammate.
- Half of the teams gather at the end line. The others meet at the center.
- The offensive partner holds the ball straight out in front with the arms extended.
- The offensive partner moves the ball slowly from right to left while walking in a straight line to half court.
- The defense is in the proper defensive stance but with their arms held behind the back.
- The defense places the forehead against the ball.
- The forehead must maintain contact with the ball at all times.
- Switch positions each time a group has reached half court.

OPTIONAL: Authorize O1 to have two basketballs. Each time a different ball is stuck out, the defender will quickly slide over and touch the ball with the hand.

SLIDE WAVE – WIDE

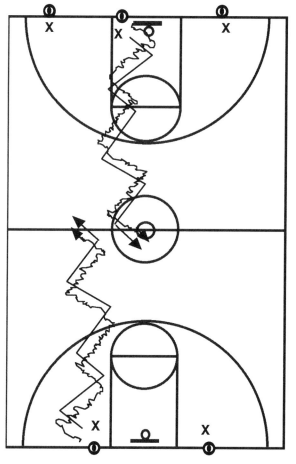

Primary Skill: Defense

Objective: To develop defensive
positioning while guarding the ball.

Equipment Needed: One ball
for every two players.

Coaching Tips to Players: It is
important that the offense works
the defense so that skill development is maximized.

© 1999 by Parker Publishing Company

Procedure:

- Each player picks a partner with approximately the same quickness.
- Half of the teams rendezvous at the end line. The others gather at the center.
- The offense dribbles under control and at about half speed to half court. The objective is to work the defender.
- The dribbler may travel a distance of only five feet in either direction.
- The defense forces the offense to change direction by playing against the ball and not the person.
- The defender may not steal the ball.
- The defender will place the hands behind the back.
- Switch positions each time a group has gone past half court.

OPTIONAL: Allow the defense to place the hands in the proper location.

OPTIONAL: Permit the defender to harass the dribbler.

SMOTHERED

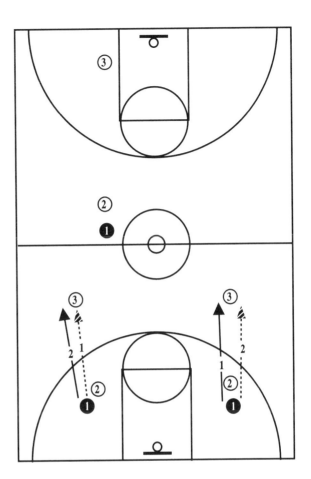

Primary Skill: Defense

Objective: To develop a proper closeout when the dribbler picks up the ball.

Equipment Needed: One basketball for each group.

Coaching Tips to Players: Exert extreme pressure by getting very close to the player with the ball. Remember, they can no longer dribble.

Diagram Notes: Upper court illustrates the drill with the players positioned at an increased distance.

Procedure:

- Players break into groups of three.
- This is a continuous drill.
- O1 and O3 will stand approximately ten feet apart.
- O1 passes the ball to O3, follows the pass, and puts extreme pressure on O3.
- O2 plays defense on O1. After O1 passes and moves past, O2 waits and will receive the ball from O3.
- O3 receives the ball from O1, bounces the ball twice, picks up the dribble, and passes the ball to O2. Next, O3 sprints to close out against O2.
- Lob passes that are higher than the outstretched arms of the defender are not allowed.
- Repeat so that each player closes out eight times.

OPTIONAL: Increase the distance in between that of O1 and O3.

SOS

Primary Skill: Defense

Objective: To develop the ability to aid any teammate who has been defeated by the dribble.

Equipment Needed: One basketball.

Coaching Tips to Players: Stop the dribbler.

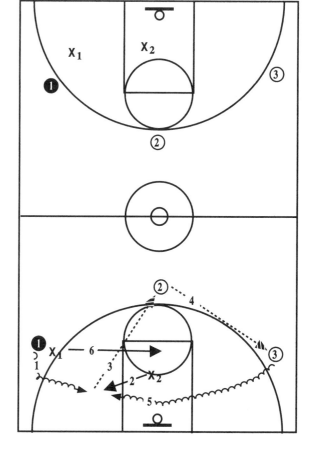

Procedure:

- Players form groups of five.
- This is a continuous drill.
- O1 dribbles past X1, passes to O2 after X2 stops the dribble, and returns back to the start position.
- O2 receives the pass from O1 and relays the ball to O3.
- O3 receives the ball from O2, dribbles past X2 until X1 stops the dribble, passes back to O2, and returns to the start position.
- X1 and X2 switch back and forth while giving help and attempting to stop the dribbler when their teammate is beaten.
- Rotate players clockwise after each defender has made four stops.

OPTIONAL: Allow the offense to attempt to score on a given signal or if and when they beat the defender.

SPREAD PASSES

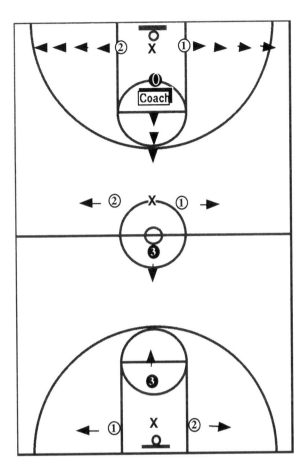

Primary Skill: Defense

Objective: To develop the ability to steal or deflect a passed ball.

Equipment Needed: One ball for each group.

Coaching Tips to Players:
Watch the shoulders and eyes of the person with the ball.

Procedure:

- Players form groups of four.
- The defender is in the middle and attempts to deflect, touch, or intercept the pass each time O3 passes to either O1 or O2.
- The coach or O3 has the ball and passes it to O1 or O2. Do not fake the passes when first learning this skill.
- Each time the defender is successful in deflecting, touching, or intercepting the ball, s/he returns to the start position.
- The coach or O3 takes one step back while O1 and O2 take one step to the outside.
- Repeat four or five times and then rotate.

OPTIONAL: Create a line of defenders at half court. With each success, the defenders will dribble to the opposite end, make a lay-up, and return the ball to the floor next to O3.

SWAT

Primary Skill: Defense

Objective: To rid the dribbler of the ball after s/he has gone past.

Equipment Needed: One basketball for each group.

Coaching Tips to Players: Focus on the ball and flip it out to the side.

Diagram Notes: Upper court illustrates the drill with the ball starting at the corner.

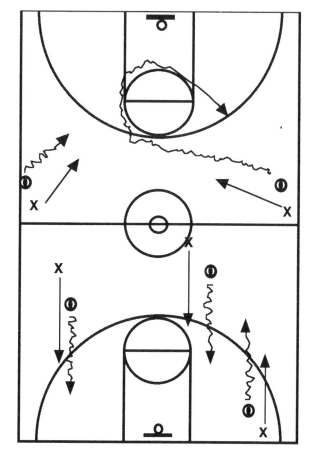

Procedure:

- Players pair up with a teammate who has fairly equal quickness and speed.
- Use half of a basketball court.
- The offensive player dribbles with the same hand as fast as possible to the half court line and then back to the start line.
- The defender chases the offensive player from the same side as the ball is being dribbled, while attempting to swat the ball away.
- Rotate positions when going back.

OPTIONAL: Use the full court.

OPTIONAL: Start the ball in the corner. The dribbler must go around the free throw circle in a clockwise direction and get back to the start line.

OPTIONAL: Place a defender on each side of the dribbler. The dribbler can use either hand or switch the ball back and forth.

TENNIS BALL GRAB

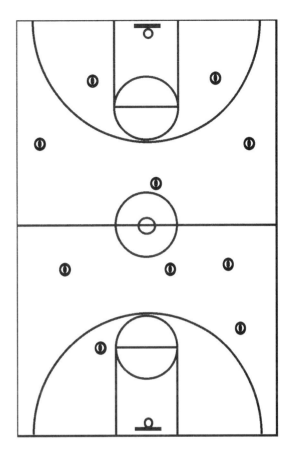

Primary Skill: Defense

Objective: To develop hand and reaction speed.

Equipment Needed: One tennis ball for each participant.

Coaching Tips to Players:
Anticipate where the ball will be.

Procedure:

- Each player has a ball and spreads out on the floor.
- Each player assumes a good defensive posture and performs the following actions:.
    a. Hold the ball in one hand and drop it directly in front to the floor.
    b. Hold the opposite hand wide to the side.
    c. On the first bounce and in as quick a horizontal movement as possible, snatch the ball out of the air.
    d. Perform a set number with each hand.

OPTIONAL: Slam the ball to the floor. As the ball is bouncing, defensive slide along with it and on a predetermined number of bounces, or when the ball bounces to a certain height, grab it.

OPTIONAL: Stand tall, reach behind the neck and drop the ball. Turn around as fast as possible and seize the ball.

THREE-D

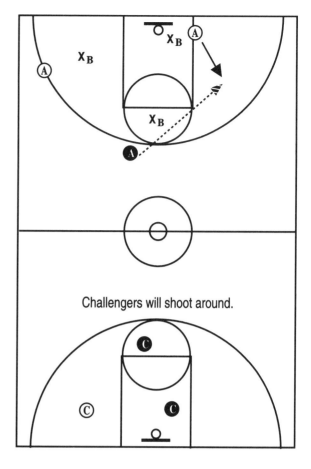

Primary Skill: Defense

Objective: To quickly make transitions from defense to offense and back to defense.

Equipment Needed: One basketball.

Coaching Tips to Players:
Stay focused.

Challengers will shoot around.

Procedure:

- Players form three or four teams.
- The game will be played half court.
- The goal is to either obtain a perfect 3-D score or score a total of five points first.
- Scoring is tabulated like tennis. One team or the other will get one point on each exchange of the ball. The ball is taken beyond the three point arc to initiate play.
- The offense gets one point for a made basket.
- The defense gets one point for stopping the offense from scoring.
- A perfect 3-D score occurs when three points are scored in a row. This could be defense, to offense, back to defense or it could be from offense to defense or back to offense.
- The winning team stays and takes on the challengers.

OPTIONAL: Add more players.

OPTIONAL: Play full court.

TIDAL WAVE

Primary Skill: Defense

Objective: To gain control of the ball or prevent a score.

Equipment Needed: One basketball.

Coaching Tips to Players: Communicate with the other defenders.

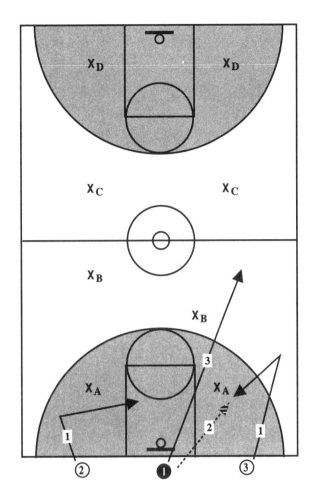

Procedure:

- Divide the court into four zones:
  a. "A" is the entire region inside the near three point line.
  b. "B" is the entire area outside the near three point line and up to the mid court.
  c. "C" is entire space from the mid court to the far three point line.
  d. "D" is the entire territory inside the far three point line.
- Send two defensive players to each zone. Each pair must remain in their zone and attempt to prevent the offense from getting beyond it.
- O1, O2, and O3 will advance the ball to the far zone, attempt to score a basket, grab the ball, return through each zone, and finally score at the near end.
- Rotate all players and begin again.

OPTIONAL: Only allow two players to be on offense.

OPTIONAL: A defensive player may go into any bordering zone.

TRAP SHOOTER

Primary Skill: Defense

Objective: To create a double team on the ball.

Equipment Needed: One basketball.

Coaching Tips to Players:
One of the defenders will grab the side of the pants of their teammate. This will not allow the offensive player to step through the trap as easily.

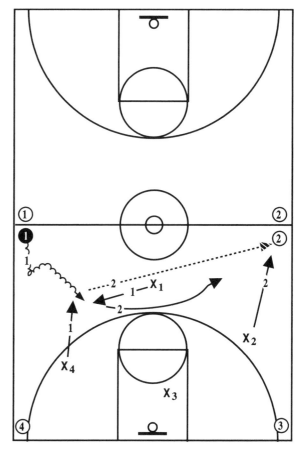

Procedure:

- Players spread out on a half-court playing area.
- O1 will have ten seconds to try and dribble into the foul circle. Whether successful or not, O1 will then pass the ball to O2 and return home.
- X1 and X4 will work together to trap O1.
- O2 will do the same as O1 and then pass the ball to O3.
- X1 and X2 will trap O2.
- X2 and X3 will trap O3.
- X3 and X4 will trap O4.
- Play is continuous.
- Switch from offense to defense after the ball has gone full circle twice.

OPTIONAL: Use the full court and place two more offensive players at the far end. Each player will try to dribble into the closest circle.

TURN AND BURN

Primary Skill: Defense

Objective: To develop speed in recovery on defense.

Equipment Needed: Six floor cones.

Coaching Tips to Players: Turn quickly and sprint.

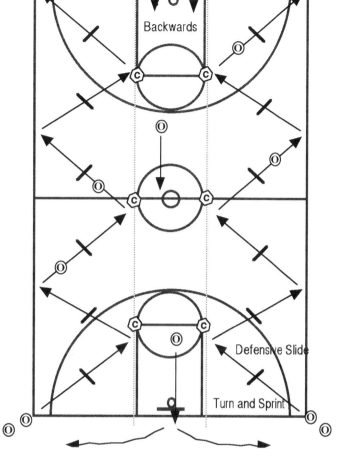

Procedure:

- Divide the court into three lanes with the use of the floor cones.

- Players will sprint the first half of the lane and then defensive slide the other half to the lane line. Once at the lane line, players will turn in the other direction and sprint and slide as before. Repeat this process several times to the far end.

- Once at the far end, players will go to the center lane and run backwards to half court. Upon passing it, they will turn and sprint on in.

- Switch lines and repeat.

- Make two complete circuits.

OPTIONAL: Reverse the course by having the players sprint to the far end, then return by defensive sliding and backpedaling in a zig zag manner.

OPTIONAL: Each player has a basketball while on the course. Have each one speed dribble forward when returning back via the center lane.

ZORRO

Primary Skill: Defense

Objective: To develop footwork for quick forward and backward movement.

Equipment Needed: Two floor cones for each pair.

Coaching Tips to Players:
Push hard with the back foot when going forward. Push hard with the front foot when going backwards.

Foot Positioniong

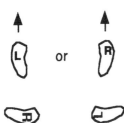

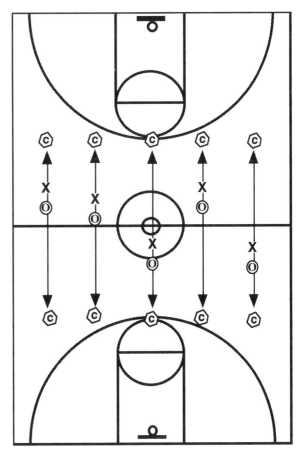

Procedure:

- Players pair up, set the cones, and stand about five feet apart.

- Participants next assume a fencing stance. (See the above illustration.)

- O1 and O2 work together going forward and backward. O1 is allowed to travel only ten feet before a direction change is required.

- After the technique is learned, O1 attempts to close or lengthen the distance between the teammate by more than five feet.

- The defender attempts to maintain the five-foot distance.

- After one minute, players switch roles.

OPTIONAL: Give each athlete a four-foot piece of foam pipe insulation. This material is cheap and can readily be purchased at any hardware store. Have the two players simulate the stance and foot movements of fencing. The target is the body only and not the head. Players may travel only 15 feet in either direction.

Section 5

DRIBBLING

Well done is better than well said.

—Benjamin Franklin

ACE

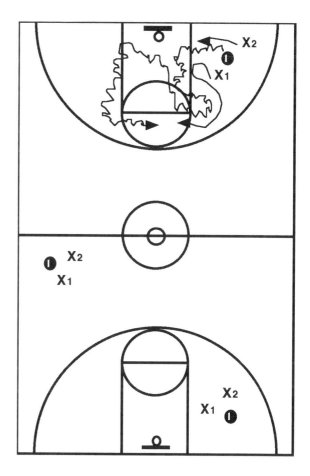

Primary Skill: Dribbling

Objective: To develop dribbling skills under intense pressure.

Equipment Needed: One ball for each group.

Coaching Tips to Players:
Try anything to get free and clear.

Procedure:

- Players form groups of three.
- The boundaries are to be decided upon by the players involved. Half court, three point area, and half of a volleyball court are a few choices.
- O1 attempts to dribble the ball for a set amount of time without the defenders causing a turnover.
- The defenders attempt to make the ball handler do one of the following:
  a. Go out of bounds.
  b. Lose control of the ball.
  c. Pick up their dribble.
  d. Steal the ball on the dribble.
- Rotate players every turnover or set amount of time.

OPTIONAL: Add one more defensive and offensive player.

BACK JACK

Primary Skill: Dribbling

Objective: To improve ball control while dribbling backwards.

Equipment Needed: One ball for each player.

Coaching Tips to Players: Stay focused.

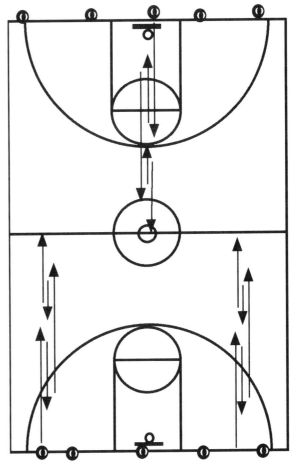

Procedure:

- Each player has a ball.
- Participants gather into two groups with one group on each end of the court.
- Players will always face toward the center.
- Players dribble the ball toward the center court line.
- Every time the coach blows the whistle, all dribblers stop their forward movement and begin dribbling backwards.
- Allow several direction changes.

OPTIONAL: On the whistle, players must also demonstrate various skills such as dribbling behind the back or between the legs.

OPTIONAL: Time players to see how long it takes them to dribble to half court and back.

OPTIONAL: Players will challenge and drag race a teammate to the free-throw line and back.

BEHIND THE BACK

Primary Skill: Dribbling

Objective: To develop direction changes with the ball.

Equipment Needed: One ball for each player and several floor cones.

Coaching Tips to Players: Be ready with the other hand.

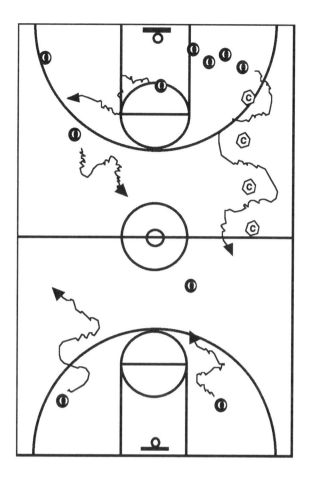

Procedure:

- Each player has a basketball.
- Players spread out around the floor.
- The coach calls out the following directions for players to practice:
  a. While standing in one place, dribble the ball around the body in a clockwise direction a predetermined number of times.
  b. Do the same as above in the opposite direction.
  c. While standing in one place, dribble the ball back and forth behind the back a predetermined number of times without an error.
  d. While walking around the court or through an obstacle course, change direction several times by dribbling the ball behind the back.
  e. Do the same as above while jogging, running, and sprinting.

OPTIONAL: Use a defender against the dribbler.

BETWEEN THE LEGS

Primary Skill: Dribbling

Objective: To improve ball handling and create difficulty for the defender.

Equipment Needed: One ball for each player and a few floor cones.

Coaching Tips to Players:
Keep the fingers spread.

Procedure:

- Each player has a basketball.
- Players spread out around the floor.
- The coach gives the following instructions:
  a. While standing with the right leg forward, dribble the ball between the legs from side to side.
  b. Do the same as above with the left leg in front.
  c. While walking around the court or through a cone course, quickly change directions by dribbling the ball between the legs.
  d. Do the same as above while jogging.
  e. Dribble the ball between the legs each time a step is taken. Attempt to do this ten or more times in a row without a miss.

OPTIONAL: The dribbler must go against a defender.

BLEACHERS

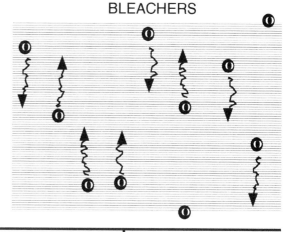

Primary Skill: Dribbling

Objective: To develop ball handling.

Equipment Needed: One basketball for each participant and bleachers or stairs.

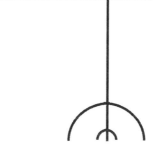

Coaching Tips to Players:
This is not a race.

Procedure:

- Each player has a ball.

- Everyone begins dribbling the ball on the floor at the bottom of the bleachers.

- On the coach's command, everyone slowly and under control begins dribbling up to the top of the bleachers.

- Stop and wait when reaching the top. When everyone is successful, begin together and return to the floor.

- The participants will perform the following:

  a. Use the right hand only.

  b. Dribble with the left hand only.

  c. Alternate the ball between both hands.

  d. Move freely up and down the bleachers without stopping.

NOTE: For safety reasons, allow neither running nor racing.

CONTINUITY

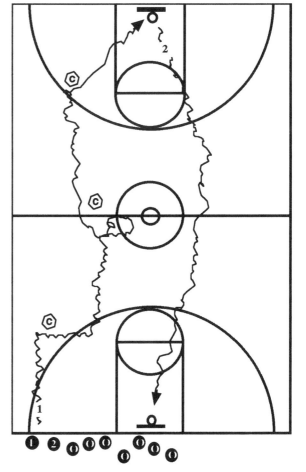

Primary Skill: Dribbling

Objective: To develop ball handling and dribbling.

Equipment Needed: One basketball for each player and three floor cones.

Coaching Tips to Players:
Keep the head up.

Procedure:

- Each player has a ball.

- Players gather at one end of the court.

- O1 dribbles to the first cone and performs a move. Once arriving at the second cone, O1 uses a second move. Finally at the third cone, O1 executes a final task, dribbles in for a lay-up, rebounds the ball, and speed dribbles to the other end for another lay-in.

- Choices can be behind the back, between legs, reverse dribble, or anything a player desires.

- As soon as O1 has passed the first cone, O2 will follow.

- Complete the circuit two times.

- Move the cones to the other side and repeat the drill.

OPTIONAL: Use stationary defensive players instead of cones.

COUNT DOWN

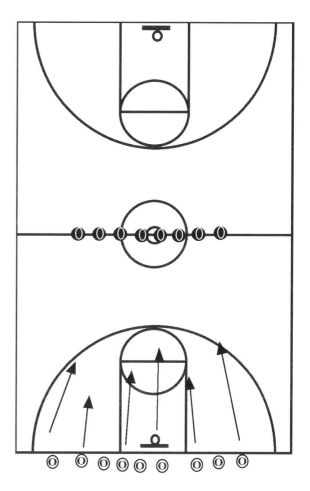

Primary Skill: Dribbling

Objective: To develop dribbling skills under extreme pressure.

Equipment Needed: One less basketball than the total number of participants and a stopwatch.

Coaching Tips to Players:
Protect the ball with the body.

Procedure:

- All players line up at the end line.
- Use only the area between the three point arcs for the boundaries.
- Place one less ball than the number of players on the middle court line.
- On the whistle all players attempt to get a ball. The one player who does not get a ball is "IT". "IT" has fifteen seconds to get a ball from any of the other players.
- "IT" will acquire a ball by either touching a ball, forcing a dribbler out of bounds, or forcing a dribbler to lose control.
- When time expires, the player without a ball is eliminated. That player runs two laps, then goes to practice skills elsewhere.
- Next game starts with one less ball and player. Work down to two players and one ball. The winner receives a reward.

OPTIONAL: Place all of the balls on the free-throw line and use only the area inside the arc.

DOUBLE DRIBBLE

Primary Skill: Dribbling

Objective: To improve hand and eye coordination.

Equipment Needed: One ball for each player.

Coaching Tips to Players: Stay focused and communicate.

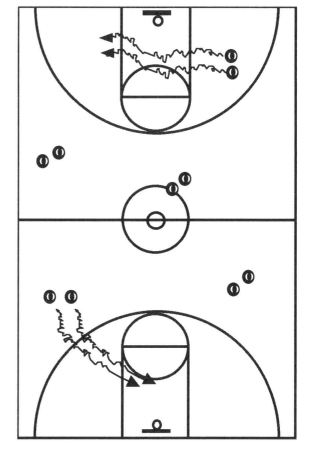

Procedure:

- Each player acquires a ball and a teammate.
- The coach will request the pairs to perform various tasks together.
- O1 and O2 face each other. While dribbling right handed, O1 and O2 simultaneously exchange their ball to their partner's left hand. They exchange the balls back and forth ten times.
- O1 and O2 stand back to back. While dribbling right handed, O1 and O2 simultaneously exchange their ball to their partner's left hand. They exchange the balls back and forth ten times.
- O1 and O2 next hook arms and dribble around the court at various speeds. They then switch hooked arms and continue. They can also attempt to switch basketballs or try backing up together.

OPTIONAL: Add a third person to the above stunts.

DRIBBLE DRIVE

Primary Skill: Dribbling

Objective: To develop dribbling and change in direction.

Equipment Needed: Five cones and four basketballs.

Coaching Tips to Players: Keep the ball below the waist when dribbling.

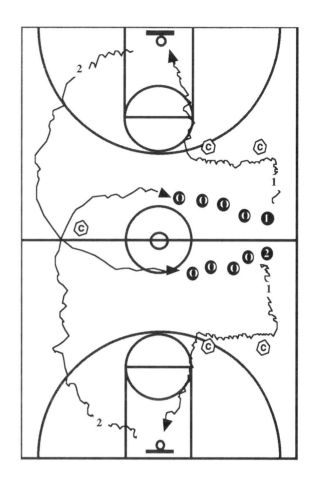

Procedure:

- Players form two lines at middle court.

- The first two players in each line have a ball.

- O1 dribbles to the first cone, makes a move, dribbles to the second cone and executes a second move, then drives for a lay-in. Next, O1 speed dribbles out around the center cone to the rear of the other line. Once reaching it, O1 passes the ball to the front person.

- O2 does the exact same routine as O1 but on the opposite end of the court.

- Combinations might be to:
    a. Switch hands.
    b. Dribble behind the back.
    c. Dribble between the legs.
    d. Reverse pivot.

ESCAPE FROM ALCATRAZ

Primary Skill: Dribbling

Objective: To develop dribbling skills under extreme pressure.

Equipment Needed: One ball.

Coaching Tips to Players:
Use all the techniques to get free.

Diagram Notes: Upper court illustrates the drill using four defenders against two offensive players.

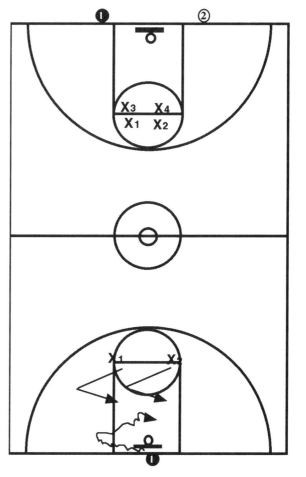

Procedure:

- Players divide into units of three.
- Use both ends of the court.
- O1 starts from behind the backboard and attempts to dribble the basketball past the half court line.
- The two defenders start from a sitting position in the top half of the free-throw circle. Neither may rise until O1 puts the ball to the floor and starts dribbling. They will attempt to prevent O1 from getting to half court.
- Set time limit.
- Alternate places every new attempt.

OPTIONAL: The defense can sit anywhere.

OPTIONAL: Use the full court.

OPTIONAL: Pit four defenders against two offensive players.

FINGER COUNT

Primary Skill: Dribbling

Objective: To develop dribbling skills without looking at the ball.

Equipment Needed: One ball for each player.

Coaching Tips to Players: Focus on the coach's raised hand.

Procedure:

- Players go to the end of the court.
- Each player will need a basketball.
- The coach starts at the three point arc and faces the players. Next the coach begins backing up, zig zagging, and reversing directions.
- The coach holds one hand high and raises and lowers various numbers of fingers.
- Each player must mirror the movements of the coach while dribbling the ball.
- Players must also watch the coach's hand and shout out the correct number of fingers being displayed.
- Go slowly at first then pick up the pace.

OPTIONAL: Various players may lead the group.

OPTIONAL: Use the gloves and glasses. (See the "Gloves And Glasses" drill this section.)

GAUNTLET

Primary Skill: Dribbling

Objective: To protect the ball while dribbling.

Equipment Needed: Two or three balls.

Coaching Tips to Players:
Keep the head up, ball low, and the hand spread.

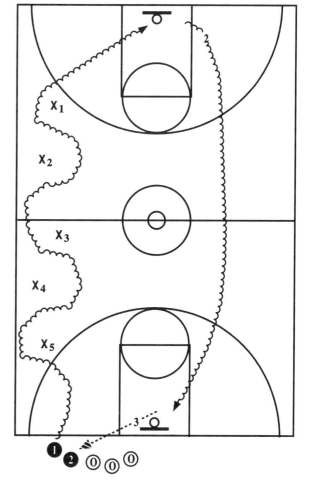

Procedure:

- Players divide into two groups.

- One group is at the end line and the other group is spread out at 15- to 20-foot intervals.

- The defense stands stationary, reaches the hands out and attempts to deflect the ball as the offensive players dribble by.

- The offense dribbles the ball near the defensive players, then makes a lay-in at the far basket. Next they speed dribble to the other end for a lay-in.

- After the offensive players have gone a couple of times, they switch places with the defenders.

OPTIONAL: Cones may be placed a given distance on each side of every defensive person. The dribbler must dribble between the cones. The defenders can play tough defense but must remain between the cones.

GLASSES AND GLOVES

Primary Skill: Dribbling

Objective: To develop hand control on the ball.

Equipment Needed: One pair of gloves, one pair of glasses, and a basketball for each player. Several floor cones may also be useful.

Coaching Tips to Players: Concentrate on where the ball is at all times.

Procedure:

- Each player has a ball to dribble.
- Each wears a pair of thick gardening gloves.
- Each wears a pair of glasses that have had the lenses taken out and the bottom halves have masking tape placed across them. This makes it very difficult to look down and see the ball while dribbling it.
- If quantities are a problem, have the players share or take turns.
- With the gloves and glasses on, the players dribble about freely.
- With the gloves and glasses on, the players dribble around the floor cones or through an obstacle course.

OPTIONAL: Have challenge drag races between two players at a predetermined distance.

OPTIONAL: Players may also wear the gloves during any phase of practice, including scrimmages.

I C U R   LOST

Primary Skill: Dribbling

Objective: To develop dribbling skills without looking at the ball.

Equipment Needed: One ball and a paper grocery sack or scarf for each team. Floor cones or obstacles to dribble around.

Coaching Tips to Players: Concentrate on where the ball is at all times.

Procedure:

- Each player pairs up with a teammate.
- One player has a ball and a blindfold or sack.
- O1 puts a sack over the head or a scarf over the eyes, then begins dribbling. O1 is not allowed to talk.
- O2 guides O1 around the court by giving instructions as to where to dribble. If the ball is lost, O2 returns it to O1.
- O2 can give instructions for O1 to follow such as:
  a. Stop.
  b. Sit down.
  c. Dribble behind your back.
  d. Turn two circles.
- Continue for a certain amount of time then swap roles.

KING COBRA

Primary Skill: Dribbling

Objective: To develop the dribbling skills around an obstacle.

Equipment Needed: Two basketballs.

Coaching Tips to Players: Push the ball across the body when making a cut.

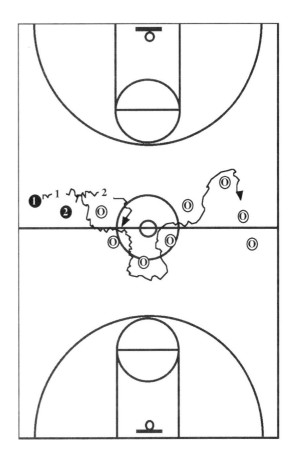

Procedure:

- All players spread out in a line with the last two players in possession of a ball.
- Allow four feet of space between each player in line.
- Players should not bump, touch, or graze any of the other players when dribbling past them.
- O1 dribbles back and forth through the line until reaching the other end. O1 creates a four-foot buffer, passes the ball back to O3, and stays put.
- O2 begins to chase O1 when O1 is about three players ahead.
- O3 begins to chase O2 when O2 is about three players ahead.
- All other players copy the previous actions to make the drill continuous.
- The snake may meander anywhere on the court.
- Continue until everyone has zigzagged through the line five times.

OPTIONAL: Try to tag the player in front.

OPTIONAL: Players must stop and change directions each time the whistle is sounded.

LIGHTS OUT

Primary Skill: Dribbling

Objective: To develop dribbling skills without looking at the ball.

Equipment Needed: One basketball for each player.

Coaching Tips to Players: Focus on the hand contacting the ball.

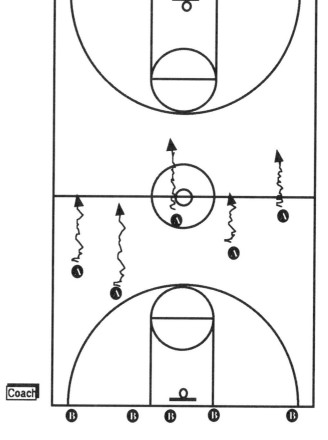

Procedure:

- All of the players have a ball.
- Players form an "A" group and a "B" group and line up on one end of the court.
- The "A" group begins by slowly dribbling to the other end.
- The "B" group must constantly be dribbling the ball while awaiting their turn. They begin as soon as the "A" group gets to half court.
- As the team is dribbling, the coach constantly turns the lights on and off.
- Players should move slowly, under control, and in the same direction.

NOTE: For safety reason, DO NOT ALLOW RUNNING.

NOTE: If lights are a problem to turn off and on, use a blindfold such as a large paper grocery bag or a scarf.

OPTIONAL: Allow all of the players to dribble at once around the outside of the court.

MIDAS TOUCH

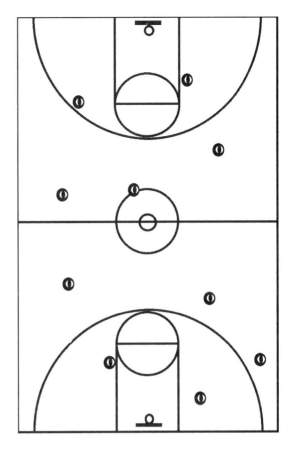

Primary Skill: Dribbling

Objective: To improve hand and eye coordination.

Equipment Needed: One ball for each player.

Coaching Tips to Players: Stay focused.

Procedure:

- Each player has a ball.
- The coach will require players to perform the following:
  a. While continuously dribbling from a standing position, slowly sit down on the floor then get back up again.
  b. While sitting on the floor with the legs spread, attempt to dribble the ball around the body twice. Do the same thing in the opposite direction.
  c. Place one knee on the floor and the other one up. Dribble the ball around the body and through the opening.
  d. While kneeling on the floor next to a wall, dribble the ball from the floor to as high up on the wall as possible, then back down to the floor.
  e. From the standing position, dribble the ball back and forth behind the back ten times. The ball must remain behind the back the whole time.

MIXING BOWL

Primary Skill: Dribbling

Objective: To develop ball control.

Equipment Needed: One basketball for each player.

Coaching Tips to Players: Do not look at the ball.

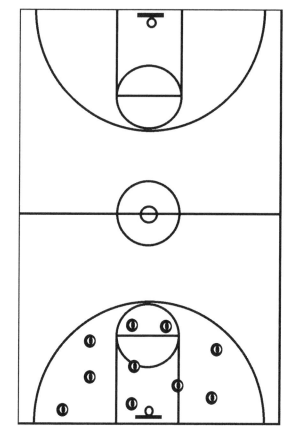

Procedure:

- Every player has a ball and finds a place to stand somewhere inside the three point arc.
- All participants must be continually dribbling and moving.
- After a short time, shrink the boundaries to the key area. Later, compress the perimeter to the entire free-throw circle. Follow this, if necessary, by reducing the circle to half its original size.
- It is forbidden to touch another player.
- Dribblers must maintain control and can not cross over the borders.
- When infractions do occur, those individuals involved will leave the inner space, do a predetermined number of push ups or sprints, and return to the bowl.

OPTIONAL: Constantly call out which hand the participants must use.

OPTIONAL: Give each player two basketballs.

RAPID RETURNS

Primary Skill: Dribbling

Objective: To improve hand and eye coordination.

Equipment Needed: One ball for each player, plus two or three chairs.

Coaching Tips to Players: Keep the hand spread.

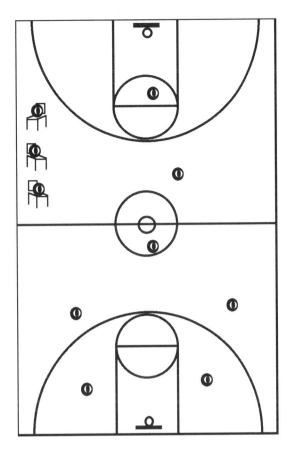

Procedure:

- Every player has a ball. Players spread out on the floor.
- Each player dribbles the ball as low and fast as possible using the
    a. Right hand.
    b. Left hand.
    c. Alternate hands - R, L, R, L, R....
- Each player performs the above skills while:
    a. Bent over at the waist.
    b. Sitting in a chair.
    c. One knee touching the court.
    d. Both knees on the floor.
    e. Sitting on the floor.
    f. From standing, to sitting, and back to standing.

RELAY RACES

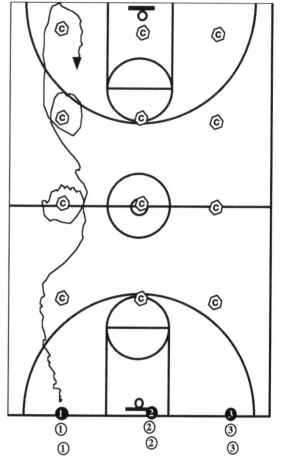

Primary Skill: Dribbling

Objective: To develop dribbling skills under pressure and speed.

Equipment Needed: One basketball per team and 12 cones.

Coaching Tips to Players: Try not to look at the ball.

Procedure:

- Players establish three teams.
- The first player in each line has a basketball.
- Any team with a lesser number, will have one player go twice.
- The coach will dictate which hand will be used for each particular race.
- Various types of relay races could be to:
  a. Dribble down and back.
  b. Dribble past, in between, or circles around cones or objects.
  c. While dribbling down, players stop and perform a routine before continuing on. Push ups, sit ups, or dribbling behind the back three times are just a few options available.

OPTIONAL: Shorten the distance to half court.

OPTIONAL: Dribble down to a teammate at the other end who then dribbles back.

REVERSE DRIBBLE

Primary Skill: Dribbling

Objective: To develop the dribble and drive down the middle.

Equipment Needed: Two basketballs and two cones.

Coaching Tips to Players: Pull the ball across the body on the reverse spin.

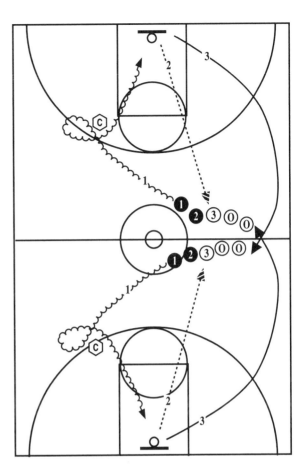

Procedure:

- Players form two lines at middle side court.

- The first two players in each line have a basketball.

- Play is continuous.

- O1 dribbles to the cone, reverse dribbles for a lay-in, gets the rebound, and passes the ball to O3. Next, O1 goes to the rear of the other line. This allows O1 to work on the reverse dribble from the other direction.

- As soon as O1 makes the reverse dribble at the cone, O2 takes off and follows the same routine.

- O3 waits for O1 to pass the ball back and then copies O2.

OPTIONAL: Place a cone on each side of both free-throw lanes. Each player is required to reverse dribble at the first cone, travel to the second, reverse dribble again, and then drive down the middle and score.

SHRINKING COURT

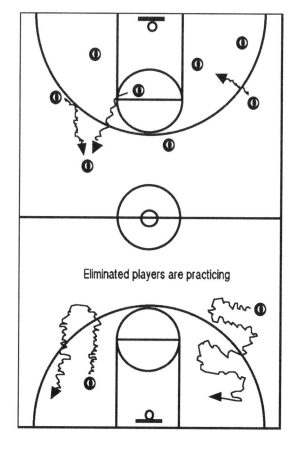

Primary Skill: Dribble

Objective: To develop ball handling skills.

Equipment Needed: One ball for each player.

Coaching Tips to Players: Protect the ball with the body.

Eliminated players are practicing

Procedure:

- Each player has a basketball.
- Everyone spreads out over the designated playing area.
- The goal is to be the last player still dribbling.
- Either hand may be used when dribbling.
- While constantly dribbling, participants will attempt to eliminate any other player by touching their basketball.
- Players do not have to be moving all the time.
- Every 30 seconds or so, shrink the size of the playing area: Start out in the half court, then to below the three point arc, next the key, the free-throw circle, and finally half the free-throw circle.
- Eliminated players go elsewhere and practice dribbling with the off hand.

SLIDE WAVE

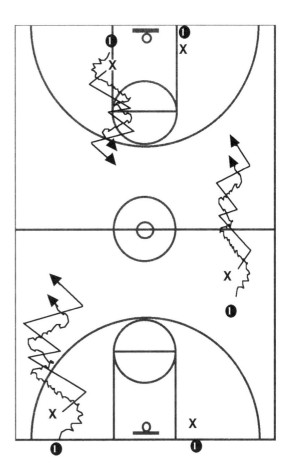

Primary Skill: Dribbling

Objective: To improve dribbling with body control.

Equipment Needed: One ball for every two players.

Coaching Tips to Players: Keep the ball low to maintain control.

Procedure:

- Each player pairs up with a teammate.

- One player has a basketball.

- Everyone spreads out along one end of the court.

- The offensive player dribbles down the court under control in a zigzag manner. If O1 gets by the defensive person, O1 must slow up until the X1 gets back into position.

- The defensive person mirrors the offensive player by playing half a person to the ball side. In other words, X1 must play directly in front of the ball.

- The defensive player should attempt to make the ball handler change directions as many times as possible without reaching in with the hands and arms.

- Switch positions at the other end of the court and return.

OPTIONAL: Allow the defender to steal the ball. The ball is to be immediately returned to the dribbler and play continues.

SPEED DRIVES

Primary Skill: Dribbling

Objective: To develop ball control while moving rapidly.

Equipment Needed: Two basketballs.

Coaching Tips to Players: Keep the head up and vary the speed.

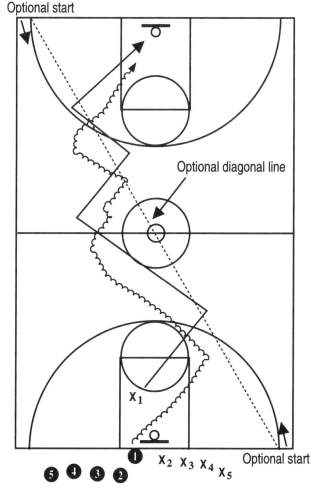

Optional start

Optional diagonal line

Optional start

© 1999 by Parker Publishing Company

Procedure:

- Players create two lines at one end line.

- O1 dribbles the length of the floor at any speed or in any manner. When arriving at the other end, O1 attempts to score, then waits at the other end until everyone has finished.

- The defender tries to steal the ball or prevent the score.

- O2 waits for O1 and O1's defender to get past half court before attempting to perform the same task.

- Players will switch from offense to defense when returning.

OPTIONAL: Cut the court in half on a diagonal. (See the dotted line in the illustration above.) Create two lines at each end. The drill is now continuous. O1 and X1 will start in a small area and as they progress down the court, the area begins to expand. Baskets are now scored on each end.

SYNCHRONIZED DRIBBLING

Primary Skill: Dribbling

Objective: To develop dribbling without looking at the ball.

Equipment Needed: One basketball for each player.

Coaching Tips to Players: Keep your head up.

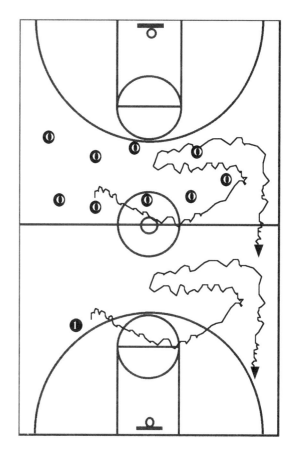

Procedure:

- Each player has a ball.
- All players spread out on the floor.
- All players will face in the same direction as O1.
- O1 will
    a. Dribble only in one-half of a basketball court.
    b. Attempt to elude the group behind by using controlled directional changes as if being defended.
    c. Stop dribbling and freeze when the coach blows the whistle. (This allows teammates behind O1 to retrieve a lost ball and regroup for a restart.)
- The other players will mirror O1's movements.
- Replace the leader every 30 seconds. Continue the drill for three minutes.

OPTIONAL: Put a defender on the leader.

TAG – LINE

Primary Skill: Dribbling

Objective: To develop ball handling skills under pressure.

Equipment Needed: One ball for each player.

Coaching Tips to Players:
Keep the ball under control.

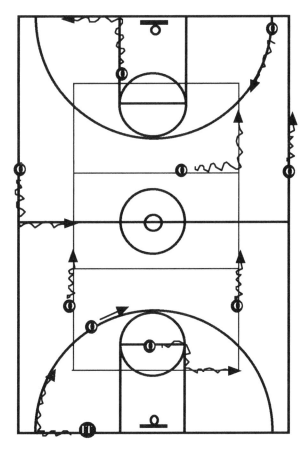

Procedure:

- Gymnasium floors usually have a variety of lines for other games. Players must step only on the lines while moving about.
- Only fast-paced walking is allowed. Running is prohibited.
- Participants must constantly be on the move.
- Players are not allowed to pass or knock others off the lines.
- While dribbling, the player who is "IT" attempts to touch another player, force them to step off a line, or cause them to lose control of the ball.
- The tagged player will go to the center circle, do a predetermined number of push ups or sit ups, then reenter the activity.

NOTE: It may be necessary to put a time limit on "IT" if the player is having difficulty with the tag.

OPTIONAL: Designate more than one "IT".

OPTIONAL: Any tagged player will go directly to the center circle and become "IT".

TAG – THIEF

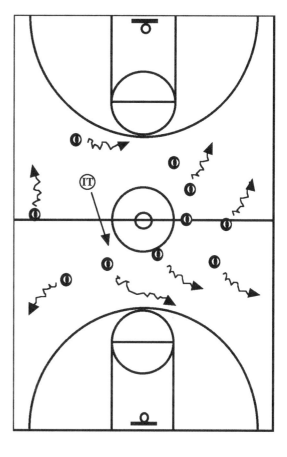

Primary Skill: Dribbling

Objective: To develop dribbling skills under intense pressure.

Equipment Needed: One ball for each player except the one designated as "IT".

Coaching Tips to Players:
Protect the ball with the body.

Procedure:

- The game is played between the three point arcs. Everyone has a ball except "IT".
- "IT" tries to make the other players:
    a. Go out of bounds.
    b. Lose control of the ball.
    c. Switch hands.
    d. Expose the ball so it can be touched.
- If successful with any of the above, "IT" captures the ball from that player who then becomes the new "IT". Play continues as before.
- Players may not tag the same individual that caused them to become "IT".

OPTIONAL: Allow use of only the right or left hand when dribbling.

OPTIONAL: Shrink the playing area.

OPTIONAL: Designate two players to be "IT".

TAG – TOUCH

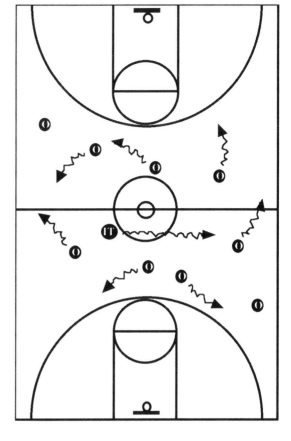

Primary Skill: Dribbling

Objective: To develop dribbling skills under pressure.

Equipment Needed: One basketball for each player.

Coaching Tips to Players: Keep your head up when dribbling.

Procedure:

- Each player has a ball.
- Use only the area located between the three point arcs.
- Dribbing is allowed only with the right hand. After a predetermined amount of time, dribbling will be done only with the left hand. After a while, give the players freedom to change hands as needed.
- While dribbling under control, the player who is "IT" attempts to touch any other player.
- Any new "IT" does the same but may not retouch the same person who tagged them.
- Try to be the player tagged the least number of times.

NOTE: If any player is having difficulty in tagging others, select a new "IT".

OPTIONAL: Increase or reduce the size of the playing area.

OPTIONAL: Designate two players to be "IT".

OPTIONAL: Any player tagged will remain "IT". Attempt to be the last player tagged.

TRUST-ME RACE

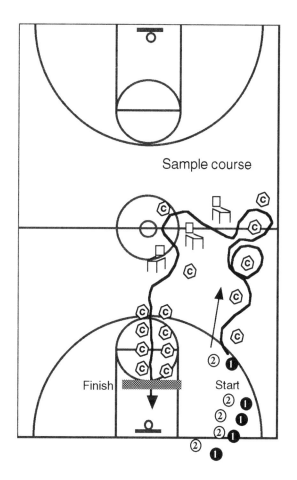

Sample course

Primary Skill: Dribbling

Objective: To develop dribbling skills without looking at the ball.

Equipment Needed: One ball and a paper grocery sack or scarf for each team, floor cones or obstacles to dribble around, and a couple of stopwatches.

Coaching Tips to Players: Concentrate on where the ball is at all times.

Finish

Start

Procedure:

- Make two identical courses similar to the one shown above.
- Players choose a partner.
- O1 puts the sack or scarf on, then dribbles a ball through an obstacle course as fast as possible. O1 is not allowed to talk.
- O2 guides O1 through the obstacle course by giving instructions as to where to dribble. If the ball is lost, O2 will return it to O1. Add five seconds to the total each time an error occurs.
- Record O1's time for each group, swap roles, and do the same.
- Add the two times together and determine which team made it through the course in the least amount of time.

NOTE: Keep the course relatively short.

OPTIONAL: Allow the players to challenge each other in grudge races.

TWO BALL

Primary Skill: Dribbling

Objective: To improve hand and eye coordination.

Equipment Needed: Two balls for each participant.

Coaching Tips to Players: Keep the hand spread and do not look at the ball.

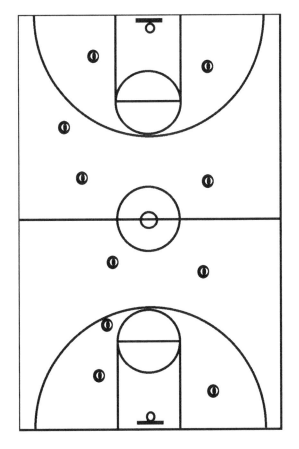

Procedure:

- Each player has two basketballs and dribbles around the gym.
- The coach will give instructions to:
  - a. Dribble the balls around freely without an error.
  - b. Do the same as above but force the balls to hit the floor at the same time.
  - c. Do the same as above but force the balls to bounce at different times.
  - d. Dribble the basketballs so that one hits more often than the other.
  - e. Dribble as low and fast as possible with both balls hitting the floor together.
  - f. Repeat the above but now alternate the bounces.
  - g. While continuously dribbling, sit down on the floor then get back up.
  - h. While dribbling, free the hands, spin a 180° circle and continue dribbling.
  - i. While dribbling, free the hands, spin a 360° circle and continue dribbling.
  - j. While dribbling, free the hands, spin a 720° circle and continue dribbling.

TWO-BALL RELAYS

Primary Skill: Dribbling

Objective: To develop ball handling and timing skills.

Equipment Needed: Two basketballs for each line.

Coaching Tips to Players: Stay focused.

Procedure:

- Players form three teams consisting of three or four players.

- Players line up at the end line. Each team will have two basketballs.

- Practice #1—Players dribble two basketballs, so that they bounce alternately, to the half court line and back. Each player goes once.

- Practice #2—Same as Practice #1 except that the balls bounce simultaneously rather than alternately.

- Race #1—Players dribble two basketballs, so that they bounce alternately, to the half court line and back. Each player passes both balls to the next teammate in line. Each player goes twice.

- Race #2—Same as Race #1 except that the balls bounce simultaneously rather than alternately.

WASP

Primary Skill: Dribbling

Objective: To enhance dribbling skills without looking at the ball.

Equipment Needed: One basketball for each participant.

Coaching Tips to Players:
Change your pace and directions often.

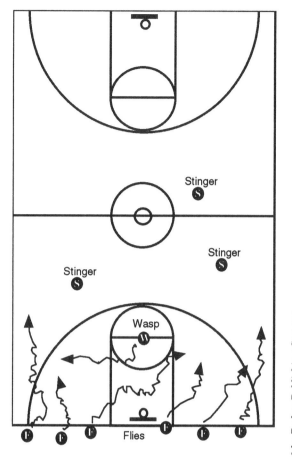

Procedure:

- Use the entire basketball court for the boundaries.

- Every player has a basketball.

- The coach assigns one player to be a "wasp". All other players become "flies".

- The flies line up on one end. On the command from the wasp, they attempt to dribble to the other end to avoid the wasp or stingers.

- The wasp starts the flies dribbling by yelling "Wasp". The wasp dribbles after the flies and attempts a body tag, a turnover, or an out-of-bounds.

- Tagged flies become **stingers**. Stingers stand in one place, constantly dribble the ball, and when a fly passes by, attempt to tag the fly with the hand or ball. Stingers are allowed to use either foot as a pivot.

- Repeat this process until only one or two flies are remaining.

NOTE: If the walls are close to the end line, use the key as the safe zone.

OPTIONAL: Designate two or more players to be wasps.

WEAVE

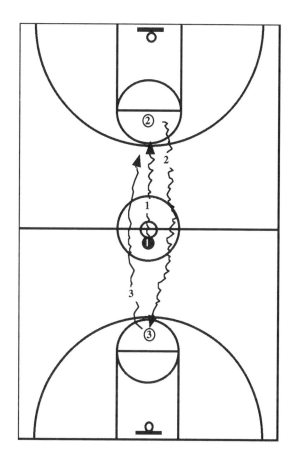

Primary Skill: Dribbling

Objective: To develop dribbling skills with a hand off.

Equipment Needed: One basketball for every group of three players.

Coaching Tips to Players: Keep the fingers spread when dribbling the ball.

Procedure:

- Players form groups of three.
- O1 dribbles the ball towards O2, hands the ball off, then takes that position.
- O2 receives the ball from O1 and dribbles toward O3 for an exchange.
- O3 receives the ball from O2 and dribbles toward O1 for the third exchange.
- Repeat and use:
    a. Right or left hand only.
    b. Alternate hand every two bounces.
    c. Behind the back.
    d. Reverse spins or pivot.
    e. Between the legs.
    f. Change of pace.
    g. Combinations of the above.

Section 6

FOUL SHOOTING

Whether you think that you can,
or that you can't
you are usually right.

—Henry Ford

100 FOUL SHOTS

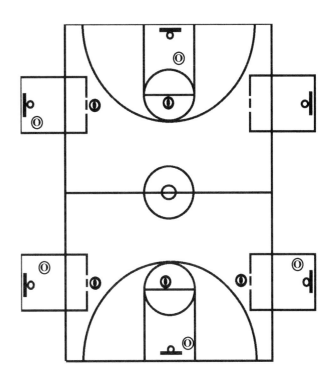

Primary Skill: Foul shooting

Objective: To improve foul shooting percentages.

Equipment Needed: One ball, one score sheet, and one pencil at each basket.

Coaching Tips to Players: Attempt to repeat the same technique time after time.

Procedure:

- Each player pairs up with another player.
- Partners go to a basket where one player is the foul shooter and the other is the rebounder.
- The first player attempts ten shots in a row, then switches with the rebounder.
- The rebounder recovers the ball and quickly returns it to the shooter.
- Record the number made out of ten each time.
- Attempt to set a personal record each time.
- Attempt to set a team record by making the most out of 100 shots.
- Try to make the most in a row without a miss. This can be easily recorded by using the recording sheet and checking off each shot as it is made.

NOTE: Make copies of the score card on the next page.

OPTIONAL: Only shoot 20 each day.

OPTIONAL: Only shoot five at a time.

100 FOUL SHOTS SCORE SHEET

Date:_____

Name:_____   Circle = Made   Slash = Miss   No# out of 10

1	2	3	4	5	6	7	8	9	10	_____
1	2	3	4	5	6	7	8	9	10	_____
1	2	3	4	5	6	7	8	9	10	_____
1	2	3	4	5	6	7	8	9	10	_____
1	2	3	4	5	6	7	8	9	10	_____
1	2	3	4	5	6	7	8	9	10	_____
1	2	3	4	5	6	7	8	9	10	_____
1	2	3	4	5	6	7	8	9	10	_____
1	2	3	4	5	6	7	8	9	10	_____
1	2	3	4	5	6	7	8	9	10	_____

Free-throw % last time checked = _____%   Grand Total   _____

Name:_____   Circle = Made   Slash = Miss   No# out of 10

1	2	3	4	5	6	7	8	9	10	_____
1	2	3	4	5	6	7	8	9	10	_____
1	2	3	4	5	6	7	8	9	10	_____
1	2	3	4	5	6	7	8	9	10	_____
1	2	3	4	5	6	7	8	9	10	_____
1	2	3	4	5	6	7	8	9	10	_____
1	2	3	4	5	6	7	8	9	10	_____
1	2	3	4	5	6	7	8	9	10	_____
1	2	3	4	5	6	7	8	9	10	_____
1	2	3	4	5	6	7	8	9	10	_____

Free-throw % last time checked = _____%   Grand Total   _____

DO OR DIE

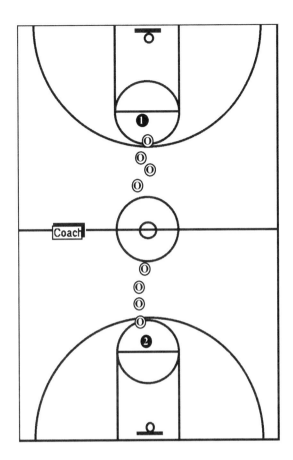

Primary Skill: Foul shooting

Objective: To develop pressure foul shooting.

Equipment Needed: Two basketballs.

Coaching Tips to Players:
Concentrate on the rim.

Procedure:

- Players break into two lines.
- One line will go to each end of the court.
- All players shoot one shot.
- The number of misses determines the number of laps or sprints to be run by the team after everyone has shot.
- Seventy percent of the number of shots taken determines the number of laps to be run at the end of the contest.

EXAMPLE: If ten players shoot, then the group is allowed to miss three shots before they begin to count for laps. Thus, if the group only made four free throws out of the ten attempts, they would have to run three laps.

OPTIONAL: Change the percentage to 80%.

OPTIONAL: Change the percentage to 90%.

FOUL-SHOT CHALLENGE

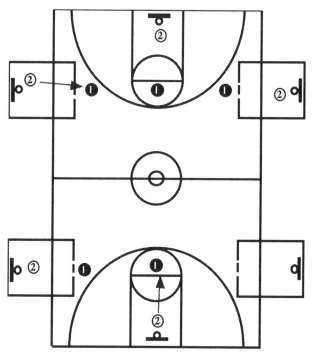

Primary Skill: Shooting

Objective: To develop pressure foul shooting.

Equipment Needed: One basketball for each group.

Coaching Tips to Players: Concentrate on shooting form.

Procedure:

- Players pair up and select a basket.
- Each group needs a basketball.
- The goal is to attain ten points before the next opponent does. An example would be that O1 needs ten points before the Kennedy High Cougars earn ten points.
- O1 goes to the free-throw line and continuously shoots foul shots. O1 receives one point for each made shot. When the shot is missed, the next opponent for the week receives two points.
- O2 rebounds and quickly passes the ball back to O1 until there is a victor.
- When O1 has finished, the two partners switch roles and a new game begins.

OPTIONAL: Change the point structure to one point for us, and three points for them.

OPTIONAL: Free-throws are on a one-and-one basis. If the first shot is made, then the second shot is worth two points if made.

FOUL-SHOT RELAYS

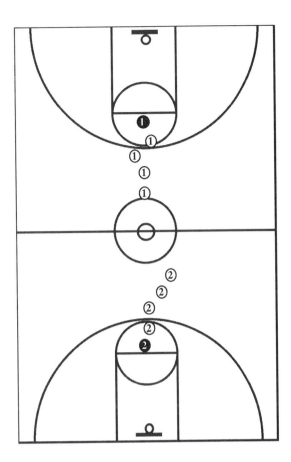

Primary Skill: Foul shooting

Objective: To develop concentration under pressure.

Equipment Needed: One ball for each team.

Coaching Tips to Players:
Cncentrate, do not rush the shot.

Procedure:

- Players divide into two teams with one team at each end.

- Play is continuous.

- The goal is to be the first team to make a predetermined number of foul shots.

- Teams must yell out the number of successful free-throws they have made each time a basket is made.

- Winners watch the losers run a predetermined number of sprints.

- Each player shoots a free-throw, grabs the made or missed rebound, and passes it back to the next teammate in line. The player then assumes the last position in line and works back up to the free-throw line.

OPTIONAL: Create more than two teams.

OPTIONAL: All missed rebounds must be put back in before the ball can be passed to the next shooter. Only successful free-throws count for the team score.

FRAZZLED

Primary Skill: Foul shooting

Objective: To develop confidence when fatigued and distracted.

Equipment Needed: One ball at each basket and four cones.

Coaching Tips to Players: Stay focused.

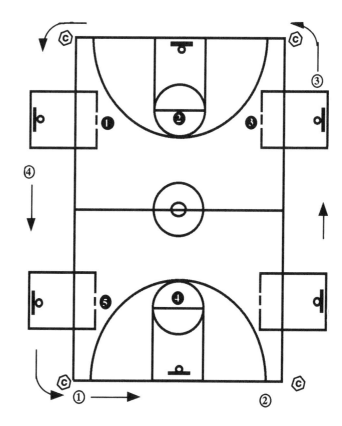

Procedure:

- Each player pairs up with another player.
- Each pair gets a basketball and goes to a basket.
- One player continuously shoots a free-throw, gets the rebound, returns to the foul line, and repeats the process.
- The other partner runs one lap.
- After a lap is completed, the partners switch tasks. The first shooter runs one lap while the first runner shoots free-throws.
- Each player must run a total of ten laps before the drill is finished.

OPTIONAL: After the entire group has finished, call out two or three players to shoot a free-throw. Each miss is worth one extra lap or sprint.

OPTIONAL: Allow a shooter of the above option to go double or nothing on a missed shot.

OPTIONAL: The team may choose the two or three individuals to shoot the extra foul shots.

GOOD NEWS, BAD NEWS

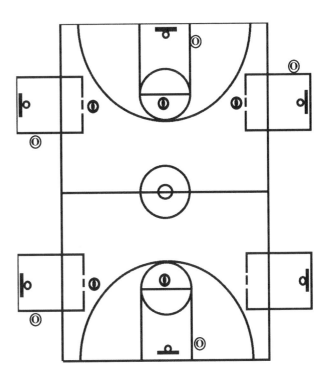

Primary Skill: Foul shooting

Objective: To develop pressure foul shots.

Equipment Needed: One basketball for each pair.

Coaching Tips to Players: Concentrate on the rim.

Procedure:

- Each player pairs up with another and gets a ball.
- The pairs go to the various baskets.
- They begin by shooting two foul shots and switching places.
- A player is called out by the coach to shoot a free-throw. Everyone stops shooting and watches.
- The GOOD NEWS is: If the shooter misses the shot, the shooter does not have to run a full court sprint. The BAD NEWS is: The entire team does.
- If the shot is successful, the entire team resumes shooting and another person is chosen a short time later.
- Continue until everyone has had one shot attempt.

OPTIONAL: Players will have to shoot a one-and-one and make both.

OPTIONAL: Allow the shooter to go double or nothing on a second shot if desired.

GROUND ZERO

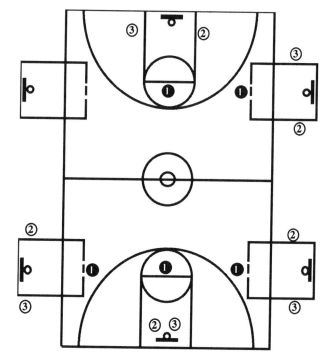

Primary Skill: Foul shooting

Objective: To improve foul shooting under pressure.

Equipment Needed: One ball at each basket.

Coaching Tips to Players: Concentrate on proper shooting form.

Procedure:

- Players form teams of three or four.
- Each team needs one basketball.
- Each team goes to a basketball hoop.
- The objective is for a team to reduce its beginning total of 11 points to 0 points.
- Each player has one opportunity to make a foul shot. If the shot is good, the team's score is reduced by one. Whether the shot is made or missed, all players rotate one position, and shooting continues.
- Rebounders must be outside the key before the foul shot counts.

OPTIONAL: Raise the starting score for each team.

OPTIONAL: If the first shot is made, the same player will get one extra shot before having to rotate.

OPTIONAL: Require all shots to be a one-and-one.

I PICK YOU

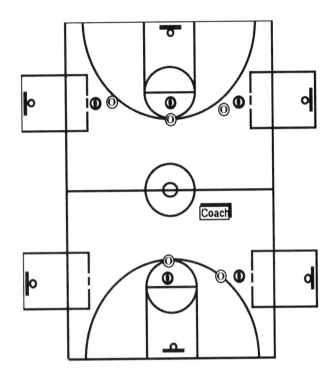

Primary Skill: Foul shooting

Objective: To develop pressure foul shooting.

Equipment Needed: One ball at each basket.

Coaching Tips to Players: Stay focused.

Procedure:

- Players spread out at each basket and begin shooting foul shots.

- The coach periodically calls on a player to shoot a free-throw. All other players must stop shooting and watch quietly. If the attempt is missed, everyone runs one lap and resumes foul shooting. If the attempt is made, the coach waits a short time before calling on another player.

- Continue until everyone has had a turn at shooting a free-throw.

OPTIONAL: All players must shoot two free-throws in a row.

OPTIONAL: A player may elect to go for double or nothing on an extra shot if the first attempt is missed.

OPTIONAL: Tally the score before running any laps. All shots are a one-and-one. When the first one is made, a second shot is rewarded. This second shot, if made, will erase one lap off the total team laps accumulated to that point.

KNOCK TWO DOWN

Primary Skill: Foul shooting

Objective: To develop foul shooting under pressure.

Equipment Needed: One ball for each player.

Coaching Tips to Players: Concentrate.

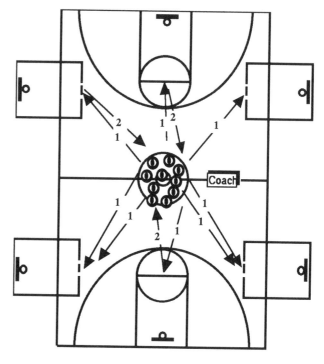

Procedure:

- Everyone has a basketball.
- Everyone goes to the center jump circle.
- The entire team begins walking in a clockwise direction.
- When the coach blows the whistle, everybody dribbles to a basket and makes two foul shots before returning to the circle.
- The order of shooting at any basket is determined by the order of arrival. If the shot is missed, that shooter must rebound the shot and go back to the end of the same line.
- The goal is not to be one of the last three players back to the jump circle.
- Repeat the drill several times.

OPTIONAL: Raise the number of free-throw shots that need to be made at a basket.

OPTIONAL: Players must make a shot at two different baskets. To prevent collisions, they must move in a clockwise direction to the next basket.

MAKE OR MISS

Primary Skill: Foul shooting

Objective: To improve foul shooting under pressure.

Equipment Needed: One ball at each basket.

Coaching Tips to Players: Attempt to attain a rhythm.

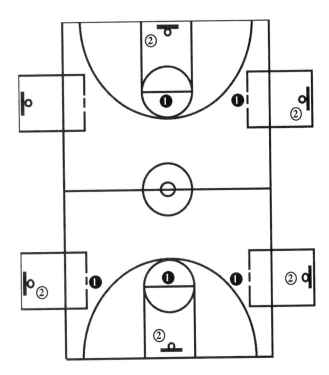

Procedure:

- Each player pairs up with another player.
- Each pair gets a basketball.
- One is the foul shooter, and the other is the rebounder.
- The objective is for O1 to shoot until a foul shot is **made**, then continue shooting until a foul shot is **missed**.
- On any missed shot after a make, both players will switch positions and continue the scheme.
- O2 will quickly and accurately pass the ball back to the shooter to establish a rhythm.

OPTIONAL: Attempt to set a personal record of made shots in a row.

OPTIONAL: Attempt to set a team record of made shots in a row.

OPTIONAL: A player must relinquish the foul line when ten shots are made in a row.

ONE PLUS ONE

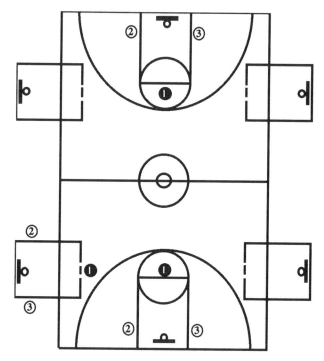

Primary Skill: Foul shooting

Objective: To develop pressure foul shooting.

Equipment Needed: One ball for each team.

Coaching Tips to Players: Focus on the fundamentals of shooting.

Procedure:

- Players form teams of three or four.
- Each team has a ball.
- The goal is to be the first team to reach a predetermined number of points.
- The first made foul shot is worth one point and allows the same player to shoot again. A second made foul shot is worth two points.
- Whenever the first foul shot is missed, the team rotates.
- Players may not be in the key when a foul shot is attempted.

OPTIONAL: Be the first player within a team to reach a predetermined number of points.

OPTIONAL: Whenever a free-throw is missed, one of the players must grab the ball and score a basket before free-throw shooting can resume.

OPTIONAL: Automatically win the game by being the first team to make six free-throws in a row.

THIRST QUENCHER

Primary Skill: Foul shooting

Objective: To develop pressure foul shooting.

Equipment Needed: One ball at each basket and one ice cold drink.

Coaching Tips to Players: Fix the eye on the rim.

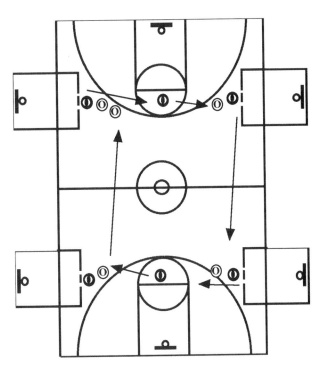

Procedure:

- Place one basketball at each available free-throw line.
- Disperse the players around the court behind the basketballs.
- Players must make one foul shot at each basket.
- Participants will rotate clockwise when a free-throw is made.
- When players are unsuccessful, they must return to the end of the same line.
- The first person to make one foul shot at each basket wins a drink.
- When a player is the only one at a basket and makes the shot, the ball must be retrieved and placed on the foul line before proceeding to the next hoop.

OPTIONAL: Shoot a one-and-one. Players are required to make both free-throws before moving to the next basket. If the first or second shot is missed, they must return to the end of the same line.

OPTIONAL: Players have to go around the circuit twice before being declared the winner.

TWICE THROUGH

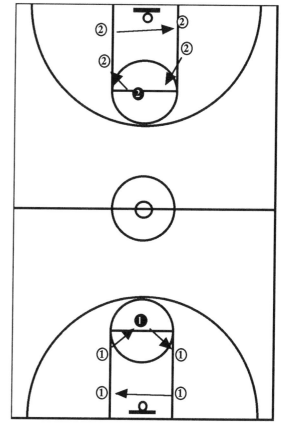

Primary Skill: Foul shooting

Objective: To develop pressure foul shooting.

Equipment Needed: Two basketballs.

Coaching Tips to Players: Focus on the fundamentals of shooting.

Procedure:

- Players divide into two equal teams.
- Each team needs one basketball.
- Send one team to each of the main baskets.
- The first team to have every player go around the key twice is the winner.
- One individual goes to the free-throw line with the ball while the other assumes proper positioning along the key. A shot will not count if the rebounders cross into the key before the ball hits the rim.
- On the whistle, the shooter will launch a free-throw attempt. If the shot is missed, the same shooter must stay at the foul line and continue shooting until a basket is made. When the shot is made, everyone rotates one position clockwise and play continues.
- The losing team must run a predetermined number of sprints or laps.

OPTIONAL: Make smaller teams and use more baskets.

TWO OUT OF THREE

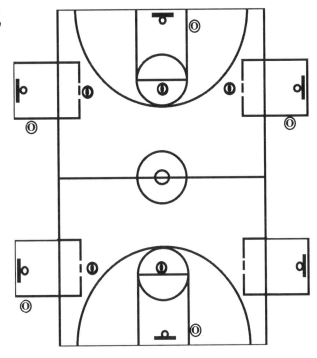

Primary Skill: Foul shooting

Objective: To develop pressure foul shots.

Equipment Needed: One basketball for each pair.

Coaching Tips to Players:
Concentrate on the rim.

Procedure:

- Players pair up and get a ball.
- The pairs move to the various baskets and begin shooting foul shots.
- Participants shoot two successive shots and then switch places.
- A player is called out by the coach to make two out of three foul shots. If successful, the entire team receives ten minutes of free practice time. If in vain, the entire team must run a full court sprint.
- Players return to shooting and another person is chosen after a short time.
- This individual shoots for nine minutes of free team practice time.
- Continue this format until a foul shot is made.

OPTIONAL: Shoot a one-and-one. Players are required to make both free-throws in order to establish the free time.

OPTIONAL: A player may elect to go for double or nothing on an extra shot.

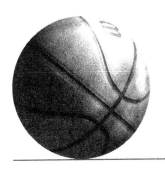

Section 7

GAMES

Nothing will come of nothing.

—William Shakespeare

AROUND THE WORLD

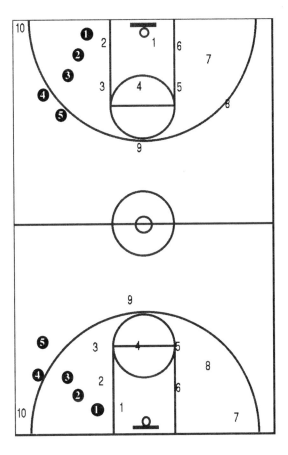

Primary Skill: Shooting

Objective: To develop shooting confidence from all areas.

Equipment Needed: One ball for each player, ten marked spots to shoot from.

Coaching Tips to Players: Learn from your errant shot.

Procedure:

- Players form two identical circuits as depicted above.
- Each player takes a basketball.
- Players have 15 tries to make a shot from behind ten spots on the floor.
- Players try to get to spot ten in the allotted number of opportunities.
- Start at spot one.
- A player must stay at a number until that shot is made.
- When successful, they move to spot two and continue.
- Several players may be on the circuit at once.
- Try to shoot when other players are not ready themselves. Ball interference could cause a miss.

OPTIONAL: Allow the players to place the ten spots anywhere they want to on the floor.

OPTIONAL: Half of the spots must be made by using the weak hand.

BASKET BOWL

Primary Skills: Shooting, passing, foul shots, and team play.

Objective: To work together as a team.

Equipment Needed: One plastic bowling pin, or something similar, and four basketballs.

Coaching Tips to Players: Concentrate on the fundamentals of shooting and passing.

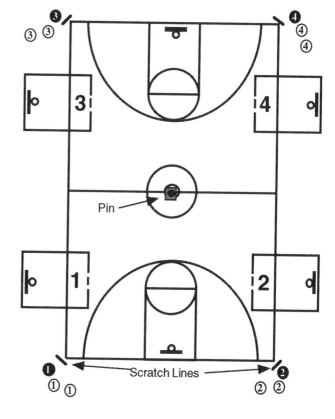

Procedure:

- Players divide into four teams. Each team lines up behind the scratch line.
- Place a bowling pin at center court.
- On the command of "Go", each team will try to knock over the pin by rolling the basketball at it. Only the participant who rolled a ball at the pin may go onto the floor and retrieve another ball. This ball is passed to the next player in line.
- The first team to knock over the pin will recover any ball and go to the designated basketball hoop and shoot lay-ins. One point is scored for each successful try.
- The other three teams will recover a basketball, sprint to their assigned baskets, and shoot foul shots. Two points is awarded for each successful try.
- The first team to make three foul shots causes all action to stop. They earn six points.
- Record team scores, return to the scratch line, and wait for the command "Go".
- The team ahead after ten frames is the winner.

BUMP OUT

Primary Skill: Shooting

Objective: To develop shooting skills under pressure and fatigue.

Equipment Needed: Two basketballs.

Coaching Tips to Players: Retrieve the rebound quickly.

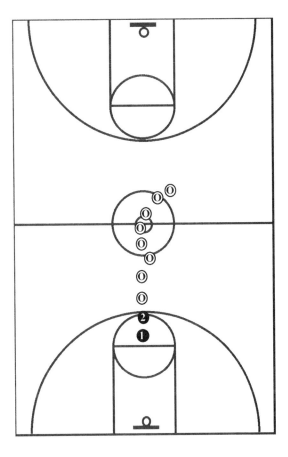

Procedure:

- Players line up behind the foul line with O1 and O2 in possession of a ball.
- Everyone must attempt the first shot from behind the foul line.
- The goal is to make a basket before the immediate shooter behind does.
- O1 shoots first. If the shot is made before O2's shot, O1 grabs the rebound and tosses it to O3. O1 now goes to the end of the line. However, if the shot is missed, O1 will grab the rebound and keep shooting.
- O2 shoots the ball right after O1. When O2 makes a shot before O1, O1 is eliminated.
- Eliminated team members will go elsewhere and practice shooting.
- The last competitor left is the winner.

OPTIONAL: The first shot must be attempted from behind the three point line.

OPTIONAL: Players may bump or throw their ball at the opposition's ball in order to keep it from going into the basket. This method requires more time to finish a game though.

CHAMPS OR CHUMPS

Primary Skills: Offensive and defensive

Objective: To develop the ability to play for positioning and get more points than the opponents.

Equipment Needed: One basketball.

Coaching Tips to Players: Communicate.

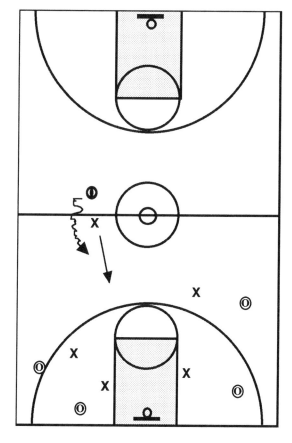

Procedure:

- Players form two teams.
- This is a full court game.
- The free-throw lane, better known as the key, is off limits to any player at any time.
- Players may reach into this space. They may not, however, make contact with the ball when it is touching the floor within the key.
- Intentionally pushing or shoving anyone into the key area will result in a foul shot and repossession out of bounds.
- Play for a predetermined number of points or minutes. The team with the highest score is declared "Champs" and the losers are declared "Chumps".

OPTIONAL: Make three teams. The "Champs" always stay and take on the waiting group.

OPTIONAL: Play this game but use only a half court. The ball must be brought out beyond the three-point arc to initiate play.

FOUR-THREE-TWO-ONE

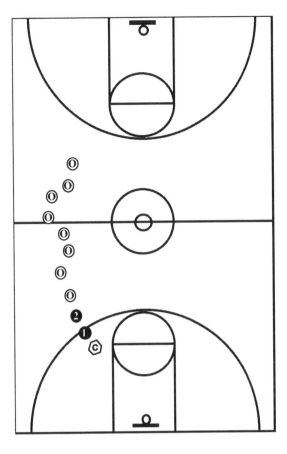

Primary Skill: Shooting

Objective: To develop shooting skills under pressure.

Equipment Needed: Two balls and one cone.

Coaching Tips to Players: Focus on the fundamentals of shooting.

Procedure:

- This drill requires two basketballs.
- The coach picks a desirable shooting spot.
- O1 shoots from the mark. If the shot is made, O1 goes to the other end of the court and practices shooting. If the shot is missed, O1 goes to the end of the line.
- O2 steps up and does the same.
- This method continues until only four players are left.
- The last four players shoot for laps. The first player to make the shot runs one lap. The second player to make the shot runs two laps and so on.
- Players change shooting sites each new contest.
- The player who had to run four laps starts the next game, third place begins second and so on.

OPTIONAL: Create two games and play two - one.

139

GAMBLER

Primary Skill: Shooting

Objective: To develop shot confidence from a variety of locations.

Equipment Needed: Ten marked spots and one basketball for each player.

Coaching Tips to Players: Use the backboard when shooting from the sides.

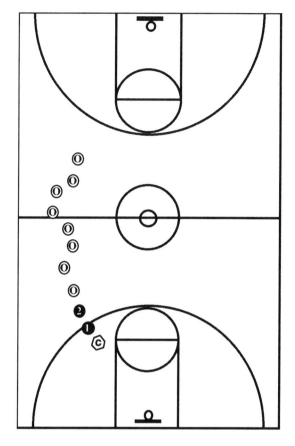

Procedure:

- Players form into two identical circuits as shown above.

- Each player needs a ball.

- Each player gets two shots at each number.

- The object is to be the first player to make a shot at all of the numbers.

- Shot options:

    a. When the first shot is made, the player moves to the next number and continues shooting.

    b. When the first shot is missed, the player either shoots again or stops and relinquishes the ball. The player begins at this spot the next time up.

    c. When the second shot is made, the player moves to the next number and continues shooting.

    d. When the second shot is missed, the player forfeits the turn and starts at number one the next time.

GOLF

Primary Skill: Shooting

Objective: To finish the course with the fewest attempts.

Equipment Needed: One basketball for every one or two participants.

Coaching Tips to Players: Learn from your mistakes.

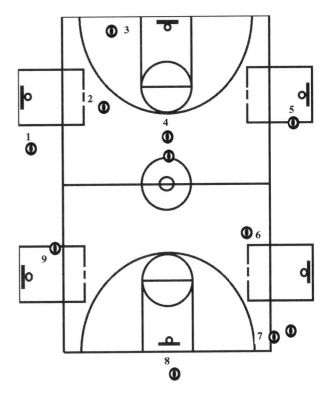

Procedure:

- Each player should have a ball.
- Design a course with nine or more different shots that each player will attempt.
- The course should be finished in a set number of shots.
- Depending on difficulty, 18 might be par for a nine-shot circuit.
- Shot possibilities:
  a. Shoot from various locations such as the corner, foul line, or three-point arc.
  b. Shoot various types of shots such as backboard, hook, or granny.
  c. Shoot trick shots such as bouncing the ball off the floor then into the basket, from behind the backboard, or using the off hand.
  d. Add a stunt prior to the shot like a reverse pivot, dribble behind the back, circle the ball around the body, or double clutch the ball.

OPTIONAL: Pair up players and use any of a number of golf formats for play.

HORSE

Primary Skill: Shooting

Objective: To make a shot that other players cannot duplicate.

Equipment Needed: Two basketballs for each group.

Coaching Tips to Players: Be creative.

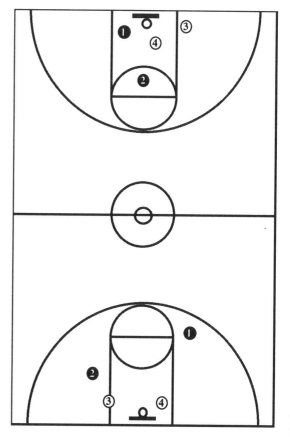

© 1999 by Parker Publishing Company

Procedure:

- Competitors determine a shooting order. The first player shoots a shot of choice.
- If the shot is made, the next player must duplicate the same shot.
- If the second player
  - a. Misses the shot, s/he gets the letter "H".
  - b. Makes the shot, the next shooter must also duplicate it.
- If that shot is missed, the next player takes a shot of choice and so on.
- Any player to acquire the letters that spell "H-O-R-S-E" is out.
- Shooters can do spectacular trick shots or call such things as "no rim" or "backboard."

OPTIONAL: Any player who is about to get an "E" may get two shot attempts to make the shot.

OPTIONAL: If desired by the follower, have the shooter prove or make the same shot again when the follower is about to receive an "E". If the shot is made twice though, the follower is out. If the shooter misses the second shot, the follower remains in the game.

HUNCH

Primary Skills: Aggressive defensive and offensive moves to get open, and shooting.

Objective: To score during extreme fatigue and pressure.

Equipment Needed: One ball for each group of three players.

Coaching Tips to Players: Concentrate on shooting and rebounding.

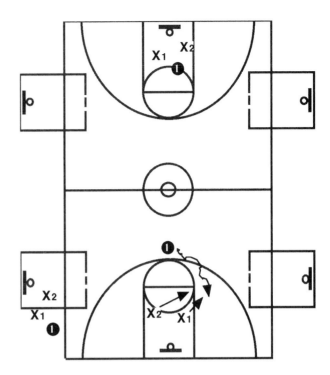

Procedure:

- Players form groups of three. Everyone is for themselves and against the other two.

- Scoring a field goal is worth two points. The player then goes directly to the foul line and shoots foul shots until missing or winning the game. The ball is playable on any missed shot.

- The first player to score a predetermined number of points wins.

- All defensive rebounds are brought out to the three-point arc before attempting a shot.

- If a shot misses the rim or backboard, it may be instantly taken to the basket.

- If the ball is turned over or taken away by a defensive player, it may immediately be taken to the basket for a score.

- Fouled players restart play beyond the three-point line. If shooting, they will go to the foul line and shoot until they miss or win the game.

MAKE IT, TAKE IT

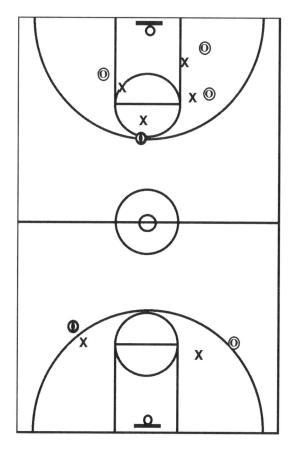

Primary Skills: Offensive and defensive

Objective: To develop scoring under pressure.

Equipment Needed: One ball for each game.

Coaching Tips to Players: Work together and communicate on defense.

Diagram Notes: Upper court illustrates the drill with teams consisting of four players each.

Procedure:

- Players form teams of two players each and play a half-court game.
- All of the rules of basketball apply.
- When a team scores, they retain possession of the ball.
- Play is restarted beyond the three-point arc each time a basket is scored.
- Each team attempts to be the first to rack up a predetermined number of points.
- The trounced team will run a forecasted number of laps.

OPTIONAL: Form teams that consist of three players.

OPTIONAL: Form teams that consist of four players.

OPTIONAL: Play a game using the full court.

OPTIONAL: Create a round-robin tournament. (See tournament section.)

OPTIONAL: Create a top-gun tournament. (See tournament section.)

OPTIONAL: Winners stay and take on a new team of challengers.

MONKEY

Primary Skill: Shooting

Objective: To develop shooting accuracy.

Equipment Needed: Two basketballs and 10 to 12 cones.

Coaching Tips to Players: Concentrate on the fundamentals of shooting.

Diagram Notes: The cones get closer to the basket the farther away they are from the number one position. Also the upper court illustrates the drill at both ends of the court using a smaller number of players.

Procedure:

- Everyone, except the "monkey", is behind the floor cones with O1 and O2 each having a basketball.

- O1 shoots first. If the shot is made, O1 stays in the first position. If the shot is missed, O1 could possibly move down the line as other players make a shot.

- The first person in line to make a shot goes directly to the first spot; the second, to the second position; and so on.

- The last person in line is the monkey and does all of the rebounding until his or her turn to shoot. The shot should be attempted from behind the closest cones.

- After a set time or number of complete sessions, the top three players get to watch the others run sprints or laps.

- Players next to a shooter may not interfere with the shot, but talking is permitted.

OPTIONAL: Divide the team and play at both ends. Top three in each group compete again.

ORGANIZED CHAOS

Primary Skills: Offensive and defensive

Objective: To develop concentration and total court awareness.

Equipment Needed: Two full courts and one less ball than the number of teams.

Coaching Tips to Players: Communicate.

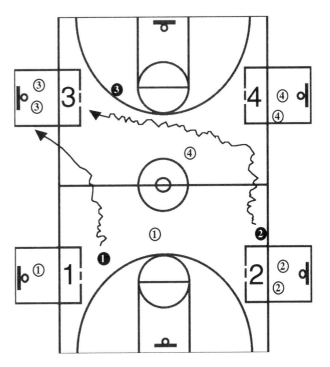

Procedure:

- Players form four teams consisting of three players on each.
- The drill requires three basketballs and all four baskets on the diagonal courts.
- To begin the game, place all three balls at center court. One designated player from each team will attempt to grab a ball at the whistle.
- Teams may score at any of the other three baskets.
- When a basket is made against team #3, only team #3 may put that ball into play.
- A team may have more than one ball on its court during play.
- The game is over when any team has been scored upon a chosen number of times.
- Winners watch their defeated adversaries run a predetermined number of sprints.

NOTE: If the teams are unequal, have players freely substitute in and out.

OPTIONAL: Make three teams and use two balls. Only courts 1, 2, and 3 are needed.

PIG STY

Primary Skills: Offensive and defensive

Objective: To develop passing awareness under pressure.

Equipment Needed: One football and a score clock.

Coaching Tips to Players: Move around and get open.

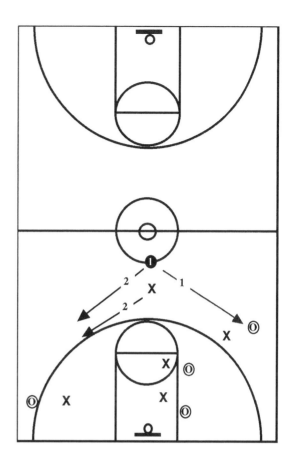

Procedure:

- Players divide into two equal teams to play a regulation game of basketball.
- Instead of using a basketball, the game is played with a football.
- The football is passed around in any manner desired.
- The football must be shot like a basketball, when attempting to score.
- Play to a predetermined number of points or a given amount of time.
- Winners watch the vanquished run a predetermined number of sprints.

OPTIONAL: Play the game at half court. The ball must be taken beyond the three-point line on rebounds or made shots.

OPTIONAL: Use any type of a ball other than a basketball. Examples might be to use a volleyball, softball, beach ball, or a soccer ball.

147

SEVEN COME ELEVEN

Primary Skills: Offensive and defensive

Objective: To develop teamwork both defensively and offensively.

Equipment Needed: One basketball.

Coaching Tips to Players: Pass the ball and move. Do not stand around.

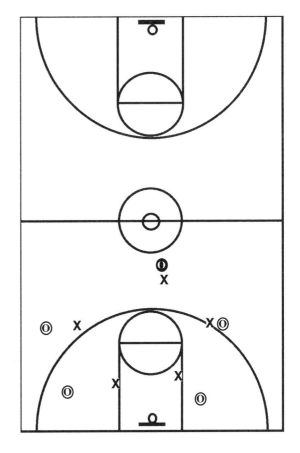

Procedure:

- Players form two teams and play at half court.
- The goal is for the offense to get to 11 points before the defense gets to seven.
- The offense will attempt to pass the ball 11 times with everyone on the team touching the ball at least once.
- Every time the offense succeeds with the 11 passes, one point is awarded.
- The defense will attempt to gain possession by intercepting a pass, causing a turnover, or creating a jump ball. When successful, one point will be awarded.
- The ball may only be dribbled on the floor for two successive bounces.
- The ball may not be held for longer than five seconds.

OPTIONAL: Reduce the court boundaries to inside the three-point area.

OPTIONAL: Dribbling is not allowed.

OPTIONAL: Authorize the defensive team to have one extra player.

SKIP ONE SPOT

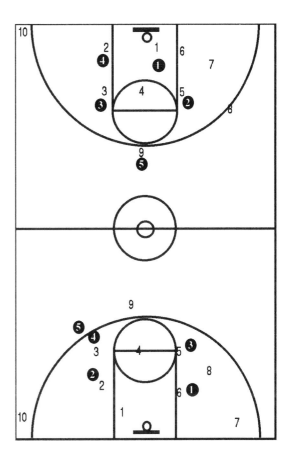

Primary Skill: Shooting

Objective: To develop shooting confidence from all areas.

Equipment Needed: One ball for each participant and ten marked spots.

Coaching Tips to Players: Learn from your errant shot.

Procedure:

- Players form two teams and play at half court.
- A player attempts to be the first to make a shot from every spot.
- The player starts at spot one and shoots. If the shot is
    a. Missed, then the next player is up.
    b. Made, but hits the backboard or rim, the player moves up one spot and continues.
    c. Made, and hit nothing but net, the player moves up two spots and continues.
- Play always starts where the last missed attempt occurred.

OPTIONAL: Allow two shot attempts. If the second shot is missed, then there is a loss of turn and that player must start over. If the second shot is not swished, then the shooter reverts back one spot and continues shooting. If the second shot touches nothing but net, then the shooter advances only one spot.

OPTIONAL: Players will go to ten and back to one before winning a game.

TEXAS SHOOTOUT

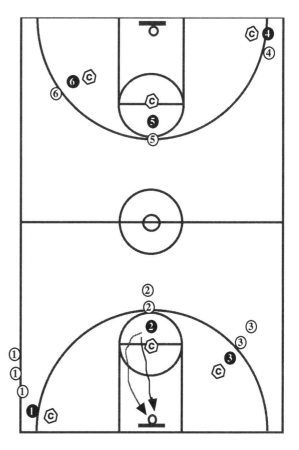

Primary Skills: Shooting, rebounding, passing, and team play.

Objective: To create a pressure playing atmosphere.

Equipment Needed: One basketball and cone for each team.

Coaching Tips to Players: Quickly retrieve the rebound and pass it to the next person.

Diagram Notes: Upper court illustrates the drill with six teams.

Procedure:

- Players divide into three equal teams.
- Each team should line up behind their cone.
- The lead player will shoot the ball, get the rebound, pass it to the next person in line, and go back to the end of the same line.
- The first team to score ten baskets wins.
- Each team will yell out the total number of shots made each time a basket is good. This creates added anxiety for the competitors, especially when the scores are close.
- Players may not intentionally interfere with the other basketballs.
- Rotate shooting slots each new game.
- Whipped teams will run laps or sprints.

OPTIONAL: Make five or six smaller teams and use both ends of the court.

THUNDER BALL

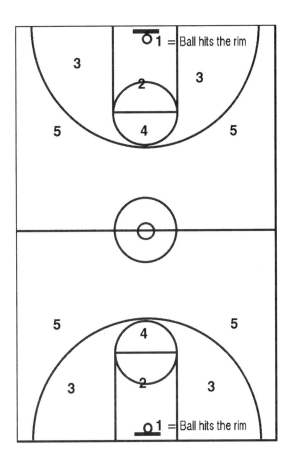

Primary Skills: Offensive and defensive

Objective: To create success for scoring and rebounding.

Equipment Needed: Score keeper and a basketball.

Coaching Tips to Players: Never give up since a large number of points can be scored quickly.

Procedure:

- Players form two equal teams with three, four, or five players on each.
- Except for scoring, all of the rules of basketball apply.
- Scoring is as follows:
  a. One point is awarded for each shot attempt or missed foul shot that hits the rim. Points are not awarded for a ball bouncing around on the rim two or three times. If a player grabs several offensive rebounds in a row and hits the rim each time, then a point is awarded each time the ball initially touches the rim.
  b. Two points—A shot made inside the lane or a made foul shot.
  c. Three points—A shot made inside the regulation three-point line.
  d. Four points—A shot made behind the foul line, yet inside the half circle.
  e. Five points—A shot made outside the regulation three-point line.
- The first team to reach a set number of points or to be ahead after a given amount of time will be declared the winners.

TIPS

Primary Skills: Shooting, rebounding, passing, and teamwork.

Objective: To get to 11 or 21 points first.

Equipment Needed: One basketball for each game.

Coaching Tips to Players: Stay focused.

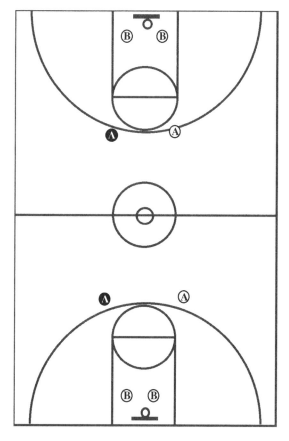

Procedure:

- Players form teams of two players each. Team "A" goes to the three-point line and team "B" assumes the key area.

- The game is scored like table tennis in that shooters and rebounders switch places after five points have been scored. Example: Team "A" = 4 and Team "B" = 1.

- Team "A" shoots a three pointer. If the basket is made, they receive one point and shoot again. Team "A" members alternate three-point attempts.

- Team "B" rebounds. If any shot by team "A" is missed, team "B" has three attempts to tip the ball into the basket. Team "B" may tip the ball to each other to get a closer tip but may never be touching the floor when in possession of the ball. If the shot is made within the three tips, team "B" receives one point. If team "B" misses the tip, then team "A" gets the ball back and the score stays the same.

OPTIONAL: Change the shooting distance.

TOP GUN

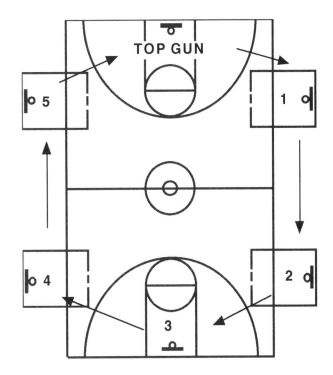

Primary Skills: Offensive and defensive

Objective: To play team basketball.

Equipment Needed: One ball for each court.

Coaching Tips to Players: Concentrate on playing great defense.

Procedure:

- One, two, or three players may be on a team.
- Boundaries are a half-court floor, but all six baskets must be used.
- The first possession is determined by a do-or-die foul shot.
- Defensive rebounds from the iron or glass must be returned beyond the three-point line before the next shot can be attempted.
- Air balls and steals may immediately be taken to the basket for a shot by the defensive team.
- The first team to score a predetermined number of points is declared the winner. Winners advance to the next court. The defeated stay and play the next challengers.
- No player may score more than two baskets in a row.
- Any team that loses at the TOP GUN court starts over at court number one.

NOTE: It may be necessary to speed games up if other teams are waiting for a challenger.

TWENTY-ONE

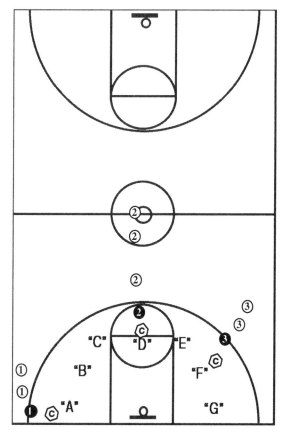

Primary Skills: Shooting, following the shot, rebounding, and team play.

Objective: To develop offensive rebounding by following the shot.

Equipment Needed: One basketball and one cone for each team.

Coaching Tips to Players: Shoot and then move to the basket.

Procedure:

- Players divide into three teams.
- Teams are to shoot the ball from a designated area. A made field goal is worth two points. If the shooter can grab the missed shot rebound before it touches the floor, and with only one step make the second shot, one point is awarded.
- The shooter rebounds the ball and passes it back to the next teammate in line.
- The first team to score exactly 21 points is declared the champion.
- Teams move to different shooting zones at the beginning of each new game.
- Intentionally interfering with the other basketballs is not allowed.
- Teams will yell out their new score each time a goal is made to let everyone know the score.

OPTIONAL: Any team that hits exactly 7 or 15, must subtract five points from their score and continue.

TWO-WAY TRAFFIC

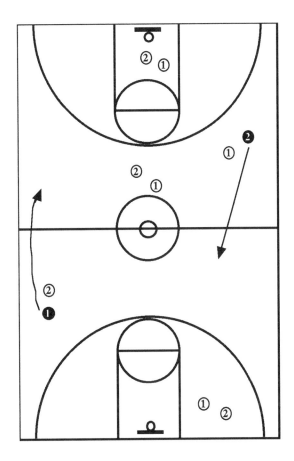

Primary Skills: Offensive and defensive

Objective: To develop court awareness.

Equipment Needed: Two basketballs and a score clock.

Coaching Tips to Players: Keep someone back.

Procedure:

- Players divide into two equal teams.
- Teams play a game of basketball using two basketballs.
- When team #1 scores a basket against team #2, only team #2 may put that ball into play.
- A team may possess both basketballs at one time.
- When a foul occurs, both teams must freeze; the shooter and any players on that end will line up for a foul shot. Play continues after the ball hits the rim or goes in during the shot.
- Play to a predetermined number of points or for a given amount of time.

OPTIONAL: One of the balls may not be dribbled.

OPTIONAL: Neither of the basketballs may be dribbled.

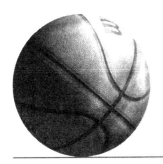

Section 8

OFFENSE

Life is trying things to see if they work.

—Ray Bradbury

BACK DOOR

Primary Skill: Offensive

Objective: To free up the wing from a pressure defender.

Equipment Needed: Two basketballs.

Coaching Tips to Players: Change directions quickly.

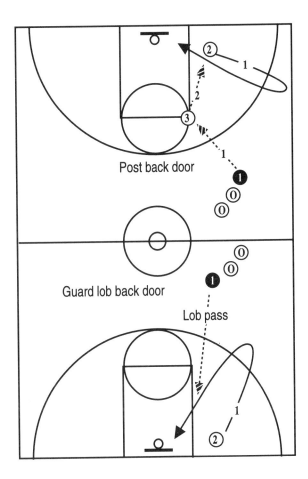

Post back door

Guard lob back door

Lob pass

Procedure:

- Players form two groups.
- Each group practices the two techniques at the opposite ends of the court.
- The first technique is the post back door.
  - a. O1 passes to O3.
  - b. O2 waits for O3 to receive the pass from O1, fakes up, goes back door, and receives the pass from O3 for a lay-in.
  - c. O3 receives the pass from O2 and then passes to O1.
- The second technique is the guard lob back door
  - a. O1 lobs the ball to O2.
  - b. O2 fakes out and up, breaks back door, and receives the pass from O1.

NOTE: A defensive person can be added but should play loose, especially when players are first learning these skills.

CHALLENGE LAY-INS

Primary Skill: Offense

Objective: To develop the ability to make lay ins under pressure.

Equipment Needed: One basketball and four cones.

Coaching Tips to Players: Focus on the backboard when attempting the shot. Do not think about the defender coming toward you.

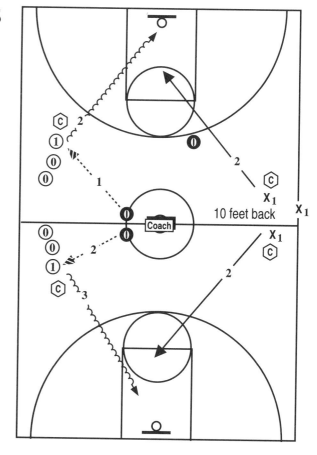

Procedure:

- Players form four lines at middle court.
- The defensive line is ten feet farther back than the offensive line.
- Players must stay behind their cones until the ball is touched.
- The coach alternates throwing the ball to the two offensive lines.
- When O1 receives the ball, O1 speed dribbles and attempts to make a lay-in.
- X1 can move only when O1 catches the ball.
- The defender tries to stop the shot from being made without touching the shooter.
- Players will switch lines and sides each time back.

NOTE: Do not cut in front of the shooter for safety reasons. Plenty of noise is allowed.

NOTE: The defensive line starts five feet farther back than the offensive line.

OPTIONAL: Allow the defense to use foam pipe insulation as in the Hatchet Drill.

CHANGE OF PACE

Primary Skill: Offense

Objective: To create difficulty for the defender.

Equipment Needed: One ball for every two players and eight floor cones.

Coaching Tips to Players: It is harder to guard an individual who is constantly changing speed and direction.

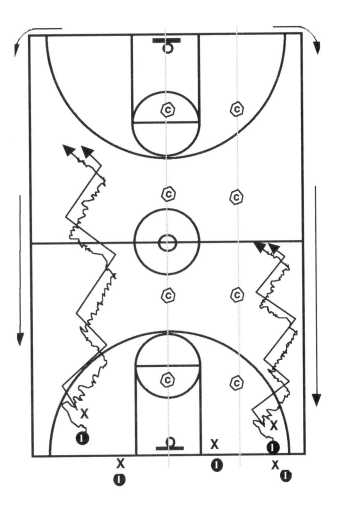

Procedure:

- Divide the court in half and then divide one of the halves again.

- All players pair up and go to one end of the court.

- Only two players are allowed in any lane at one time.

- Every player must stay within the boundaries during play.

- O1 dribbles to the other end with changes in direction and speed. If O1 gets past the defender, O1 will stop and let the defender reestablish proper positioning.

- The defense attempts to either steal the ball, force the dribbler to go out of bounds, cause a dribbling error, or make the dribbler pick up the ball.

- If the defender causes any of the above situations, the offensive player will retain the ball and renew dribbling.

- Players should go to a new lane each time they return to the start line.

OPTIONAL: When the defender causes a turnover, the roles are automatically switched.

CONTROLLED ONE-ON-ONE

Primary Skill: Offense

Objective: To develop aggressive offensive skills.

Equipment Needed: Two basketballs.

Coaching Tips to Players: Go to the basket hard when attempting to score.

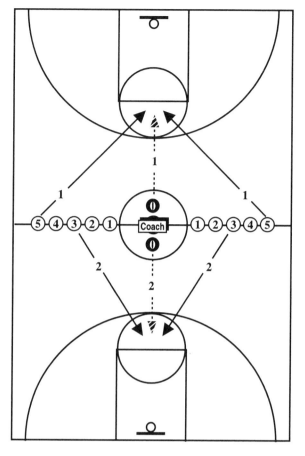

Procedure:

- Players form pairs of equally talented players.
- The coach assigns each pair an identical number.
- Use one player from each of the numbered groups to form the lines at middle court.
- The coach rolls two balls in opposite directions, calling out a first number and then a second number.
- The two players, called initially, sprint to the first ball.
- The two players, called last, hustle toward the second ball.
- Each player with a ball has 15 seconds to score.
- The other players assume the defensive roll and attempt to prevent a score.
- Play continues when the offensive player gets the rebound.
- Players switch sides when returning to the line.

OPTIONAL: At the conclusion, one lap is performed for each time a player was scored upon.

FIVE THREE TWO

Primary Skill: Offense

Objective: To develop teamwork and score against pressure.

Equipment Needed: One basketball for each group.

Coaching Tips to Players: Make good crisp passes.

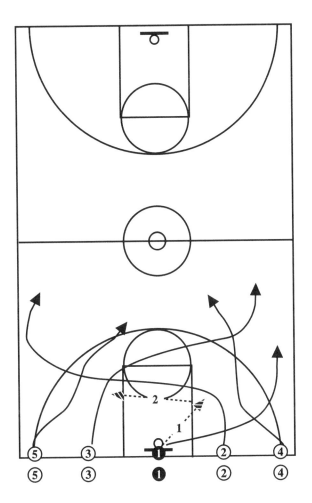

Procedure:

- Players form five lines.
- Start the ball in the middle line.
- Five players weave to the opposite end of the court and attempt a lay-in.
- The rule to remember is to pass the ball and go **behind** two players.
- O1 passes the ball to O2, then cuts behind both O2 and O4.
- O2 receives the pass, moves down court, passes the ball to O3, then cuts behind both O3 and O5 and so on until the lay-in.
- The last passer and the shooter will turn and sprint back to the starting end. These two will play defense against the other three.
- On a made lay-in, the offense must take the ball out of bounds to begin play. If the shot is missed, the offense will immediately take off on a fast break.

OPTIONAL: Do not allow dribbling at anytime.

163

FLASH MOVE

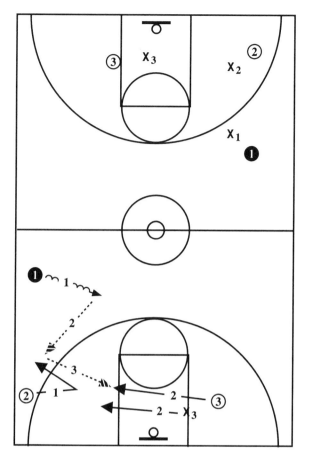

Primary Skill: Offense

Objective: To get the ball in to a post or a low positioned player.

Equipment Needed: One ball.

Coaching Tips to Players:
Give the passer a target by holding the hand up.

Diagram Notes: Upper court illustates full-defense option.

© 1999 by Parker Publishing Company

Procedure:

- Players form two equal teams.
- Each team locates at opposite ends of the court.
- Shooting is not allowed.
- O1 tries to pass to O3. If not, then passes to O2.
- O2 tries to pass to O3. If not, then passes back to O1.
- O3 flashes from side to side, attempting to receive the pass then score.
- Switch from offense to defense often.

OPTIONAL: Add a defender against O2.

OPTIONAL: Add a full defense against the offense.

OPTIONAL: Allow O3 to score after a predetermined number of successful passes have been caught.

OPTIONAL: Allow O3 to score at any time.

GIVE AND GO—CLOSE

Primary Skill: Offense

Objective: To develop the ability to get open to receive a hand-off.

Equipment Needed: Two basketballs.

Coaching Tips to Players: After the pass or hand-off, break quickly to the basket.

Diagram Notes: Upper court shows outside give and go; lower court, inside give and go.

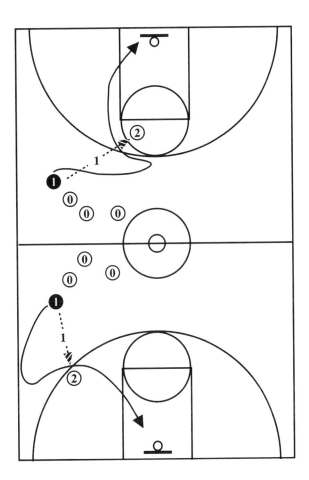

Procedure:

- The team splits into two groups. Send each team to a different end of the court.

- O1 passes the ball to O2. O1 fakes right or left, then cuts by O2 as close as possible for the hand-off. O2 hands the ball back to O1 for the shot.

- O1 should try to make a different shot with each new attempt. These could be any of the following:

  a. Lay-in against the backboard.

  b. Lay-in over the front of the rim.

  c. Jump shot against the backboard.

  d. Jump shot without using the board.

  e. Reverse lay-up.

  f. Hook shot.

OPTIONAL: Defensive players can be added after the basic skills are acquired.

GIVE AND GO—WIDE

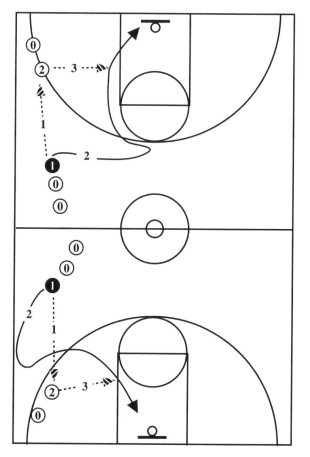

Primary Skill: Offense

Objective: To develop the ability to get open to receive a pass.

Equipment Needed: Two basketballs.

Coaching Tips to Players: After the pass or hand-off, break quickly to the basket.

Diagram Notes: Upper court illustrates the drill from the left side.

Procedure:

- Send five or six players to each end of the court.

- O1 passes the ball to O2, fakes right or left, then sprints to the basket for a return pass from O2.

- O1 should try to make a different shot with each new attempt. These could be any of the following:

  a. Lay-in against the backboard.

  b. Lay-in over the front of the rim.

  c. Jump shot against or without the backboard.

  d. Reverse lay-up.

  e. Hook shot.

- Switch lines after shooting or passing.

OPTIONAL: Defensive players may be added after the basic skills are acquired.

HATCHET

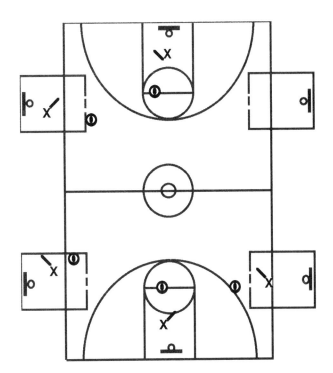

Primary Skill: Offense

Objective: To develop confidence when physically contacted by the defense.

Equipment Needed: One basketball and one piece of 3' to 4' foam pipe insulation wrap for each basket. (This can be purchased at any hardware store.)

Coaching Tips to Players: Try not to think about being contacted during the drive or shot.

Procedure:

- Players choose partners.

- One player has a ball.

- The defender has the foam pipe insulation.

- Each time the offensive player attempts to shoot, the defender hits the body and arms of the shooter with the foam.

- The offensive player has five attempts to score against the defender. This is a do-or-die situation. Only one attempt is allowed for each shot.

- Switch positions and repeat the skill.

NOTE: For safety reasons, players must not intentionally hit, swing, or poke at the head.

ONE-TWO, TWO-ONE

Primary Skill: Offense

Objective: To score against adverse odds.

Equipment Needed: One basketball.

Coaching Tips to Players: Stay focused.

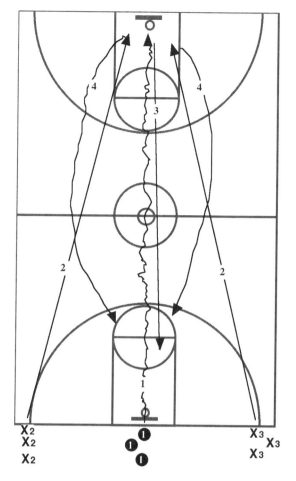

Procedure:

- Create three lines of players at one end of the basketball court.
- Give two or three balls to the middle line.
- O1 speed dribbles to the far end of the basketball court and attempts to make a lay-in.
- O1 races back to the near end and becomes X1. X1 plays tenacious defense against O2 and O3.
- As soon as O1 passes the foul line, X2 and X3 begin chasing the dribbler.
- X2 and X3 try to prevent O1 from making the lay-in at the far end.
- X2 and X3 grab the rebound and immediately transform into O3 and O4. They return with the ball and strive to score against the new X1.
- Players switch lines after returning.

OPTIONAL: Do not allow O2 and O3 to dribble the ball when returning.

PICK AND ROLL

Primary Skill: Offense

Objective: To develop the skill needed to get open.

Equipment Needed: Two basketballs.

Coaching Tips to Players: When rolling to the basket, do not turn your back to the ball.

Diagram Notes: Upper court illustrates the drill with a defender for more challenge.

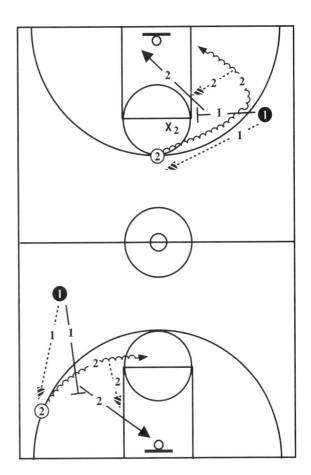

Procedure:

- Each player pairs up with a teammate.
- Each pair has a ball.
- O1 passes the ball to O2, goes to O2's imaginary defender, and sets a screen. As soon as O2 has passed by, O1 rolls to the basket
- O2 receives the ball from O1, waits for O1 to set the screen, dribbles around O1, and passes the ball back when O1 rolls to the basket.
- Repeat the drill five times.
- Switch roles and continue as before.
- The next phase is to add a third person to play defense against O2.
- The final task will be to add a fourth player to guard O1.
- Rotate positions often.

NOTE: The defense should play very loose while students are learning the technique.

RATTLESNAKE

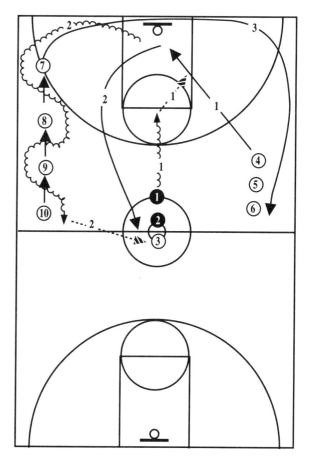

Primary Skill: Offense

Objective: To combine several different skills into a warm-up routine.

Equipment Needed: Two or three balls.

Coaching Tips to Players: Be sharp and stay alert.

Procedure:

- Create three lines of players.
- Distribute two or three basketballs to the middle line.
- O1 dribbles to the foul line, jump stops, passes to O4, gets O4's rebound, dribble weaves past O7, O8, O9, and O10, jump stops, performs a reverse pivot, then passes to O3.
- O4 breaks to the basket, receives the pass from O1, makes the lay-in, and runs up the middle to the end of the center line.
- O7 waits for O1 to dribble by, sprints under the basket, then goes to the end of the lay-in line.
- O8, O9, and O10 move forward one position each time a dribbler weaves past.
- Flip all positions after a set time so lay-ins can be attempted on the other side too.

NOTE: This can be a great warm-up drill.

170

ROCKER-JAB STEP

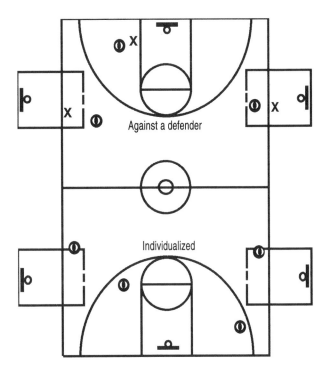

Against a defender

Individualized

Primary Skill: Offense

Objective: To develop footwork and fakes so that an open shot can be taken.

Equipment Needed: One ball for every two or three players.

Coaching Tips to Players: Make distinctive and deliberate fakes.

Procedure:

- Each player pairs up with a teammate.

- One basketball is used between them.

- One player practices the rocker or jab step and then shoots the ball, while the other player fetches the rebound and passes the ball back.

- Techniques to work on are:

    a. Fake a drive right or left, then shoot the ball.

    b. Fake a drive to the right, then dribble left.

    c. Fake a drive to the left, then dribble right.

    d. Fake the shot, then drive right or left.

- Rotate positions after all techniques have been practiced twice.

- Next, put a defender against the shooter. The defender should play loose at first.

- Rotate as before.

ROGUE'S GALLERY

Primary Skill: Offense

Objective: To get open for the shot under pressure.

Equipment Needed: One basketball.

Coaching Tips to Players: Give great fakes.

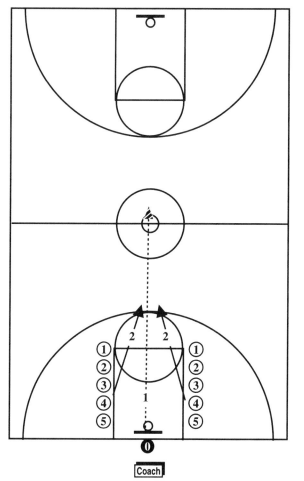

Procedure:

- Students pair up and are assigned identical numbers.

- One basketball is needed for this drill.

- Players line up directly across from each other on opposite sides of the key.

- The coach will roll the ball through the middle and call out a number. The corresponding players attempt to gain possession of the ball and score against their counterpart. An offensive rebound awards that player an additional 15 seconds.

- Players have a 15-second time limit to shoot the ball.

- All other players sprint to the three-point line and wait.

- After a score or stop, all players line up in the same positions again.

OPTIONAL: The coach may call out two or more numbers at the same time.

OPTIONAL: As soon as the ball is touched, a ten-second vocal count down is started.

SCREEN PICK – BALL

Primary Skill: Offense

Objective: To develop skills that allow an offensive player to set a proper screen.

Equipment Needed: One basketball.

Coaching Tips to Players: Make sure the screen is set before dribbling around it.

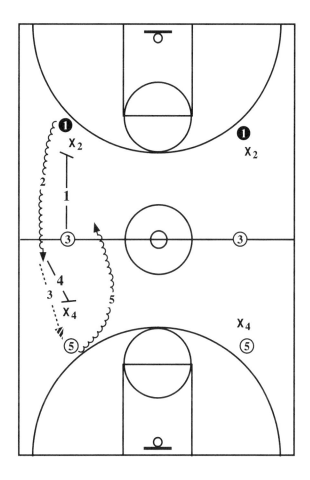

Procedure:

- Players divide into groups of five.

- O1 has the ball, waits for O3 to set the screen, dribbles by X2 toward X4, passes to O5, then sets a screen against X4.

- X2 plays against O1. After the screen has been set and O1 dribbles past, X2 transforms into O2 by assuming the outside spot.

- O3 sets the screen against X2. After O1 goes past, O3 will become X3 for the next go-around.

- X4 plays against O5. After the screen has been set and O5 dribbles past, X4 becomes O4 and moves to the outside spot.

- O5 waits for O1 to set the screen, dribbles by X4 toward X3, passes to O2, then sets a screen against X3.

- This weave is run continuously for a predetermined amount of time.

SCREEN PICK – PERSISTENT

Primary Skill: Offense

Objective: To develop skills that allow an offensive player to get open for a pass.

Equipment Needed: One basketball.

Coaching Tips to Players: Be deliberate when setting the defense up for the cut off of the screen pick.

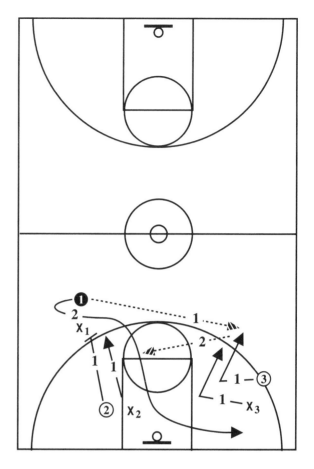

Procedure:

- Players form offensive and defensive units of three or more and report to a half-court playing area.
- Players are not allowed to shoot the ball during this drill.
- O1 passes the ball to O3, fakes one direction, then cuts the other direction off O2's screen for a return pass from O3. O1 must wait for O2 to be stationary before executing the cut.
- O3 receives the pass from O1. O3 now has the option of passing back to O1 or waiting for a screen pick to be set against X3.
- O2 is the screener and sets the pick on X1.

OPTIONAL: Players may shoot the ball after a predetermined number of screen picks.

OPTIONAL: Add more players and allow two or more players to set a screen on the same defensive person.

SCREEN PICK – SCORE

Primary Skill: Offense

Objective: To develop skills that allow an offensive player to get open for a shot.

Equipment Needed: One basketball.

Coaching Tips to Players: All cuts should be very close to the screen.

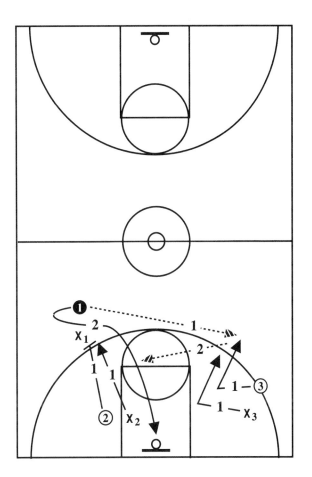

Procedure:

- Players form offensive and defensive units of three or more and report to a half-court playing area.

- O1 passes the ball to O3, fakes one direction, then cuts the other direction off O2's screen for a return pass. O1 waits for O2 to become stationary before beginning any forward movement on the cut.

- O3 receives the pass from O1, then passes back to O1 after O1 cuts by the screen.

- O2 is the screener and sets the pick against X1.

- The defense plays soft until the offense has learned the skill.

- Players rotate often.

NOTE: The offensive cutter may choose to cut right or left off the screen.

OPTIONAL: Add more players and allow two or more offensive players to set a screen on the same defensive person.

SCREEN RESCREEN

Primary Skill: Offense

Objective: To develop skills that allow an offensive player to get open for a shot.

Equipment Needed: One basketball

Coaching Tips to Players:
Wait for the screen to be set before moving.

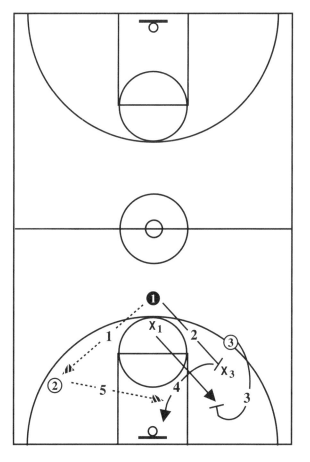

Procedure:

- Players break into groups of five and report to a half-court area.
- Each group will need one basketball.
- Set the screens at different places on the court.
- O1 passes the ball to O2 then sets a screen on X3. As soon as O3 sets the screen on X1, O1 breaks to the basket for a return pass from O2, and shoots a lay-in.
- O2 receives the ball from O1, waits for O1 to break off of the second screen set by O3, then passes the ball back to O1.
- O3 breaks off the screen set by O1 and immediately screens X1.
- The defense should play loose at first.

OPTIONAL: Allow shooting after a given number of screens have been set.

OPTIONAL: Place a defender against O2 also.

SCREEN THE SCREENER

Primary Skill: Offense

Objective: To develop skills that allow an offensive player to get open for a shot.

Equipment Needed: One basketball.

Coaching Tips to Players: Wait for the screen to be set before moving.

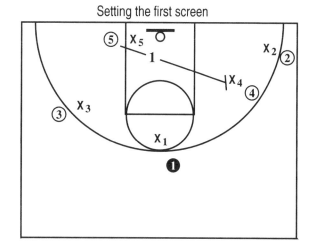

Setting the first screen

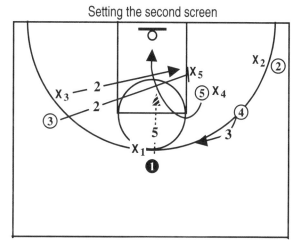

Setting the second screen

Procedure:

- Players divide into an offensive and a defensive unit.

- Only one basketball is needed.

- O1 waits and passes the ball to an open O5.

- O2 clears out of the screening area.

- O3 sets a screen on X5. O3 will arrive a split second after O5 sets the first screen against X4.

- O4 waits for the second screen to occur, then moves out of the area.

- O5 sets a screen on X4, waits for the O3 screen, then breaks to the basket looking for a pass from O1.

OPTIONAL: Do not use any defenders when first learning the skill.

OPTIONAL: Make the defenders put their hands behind their backs.

OPTIONAL: Two or more players may set the screen on the original screener.

SPLIT THE POST

Primary Skill: Offense

Objective: To score by creating mass confusion for the defense.

Equipment Needed: One basketball for each group.

Coaching Tips to Players: Give good fakes and cut close to the post player. The second cutter should follow right behind the first.

Diagram Notes: Upper court illustrates a top lane split while the lower court shows a side lane split.

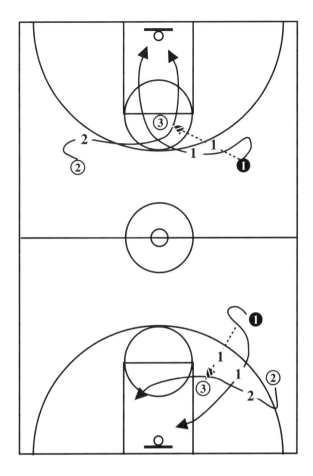

Procedure:

- Players form groups of three.

- Each group needs a basketball.

- O1 passes the ball to O3, makes a fake, and cuts by the post player.

- O2 waits for O1 to get past O3, then follows close behind O1 in the opposite direction. The rule to remember is that the passer is always the first cutter. This helps to prevent confusion and collisions.

- Timing is critical between O1 and O2. They should attempt to arrive at O3's location at about the same time.

- O3 receives the ball from O1, then hands off to either O1 or O2. O3 may also fake the hand-off, turn and face the basket, shoot the ball, or drive to the basket.

- Rotate the players often.

OPTIONAL: Add defensive players.

THREE-TWO

Primary Skill: Offense

Objective: To develop the ability to find the open player.

Equipment Needed: Two basketballs.

Coaching Tips to Players: The offensive players should stay spread apart and not bunch up.

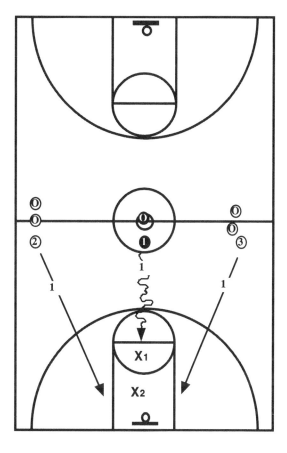

Procedure:

- Create three lines of players at center court. The ball starts in the middle.
- O1 drives to the top of the key and stops. O1 can shoot the ball or pass to O2 or O3.
- O2 and O3 go to the bottom of the key, stop, possibly receive the pass from O1, shoot the shot, or pass the ball back to either open teammate.
- When an offensive player recovers the rebound, play continues.
- The defense may rotate out when they
  a. Recover the rebound.
  b. Force a turnover.
  c. Defend against a predetermined number of groups.

OPTIONAL: This is a great warm-up drill.

OPTIONAL: Use the full court. When X1 or X2 get the rebound, either made or missed, they will work the ball to the other end for a lay-in.

179

THREE-TWO-ONE

Primary Skill: Conditioning

Objective: To develop teamwork and ball control while attempting to score.

Equipment Needed: One basketball for every three players.

Coaching Tips to Players: Stay focused and alert.

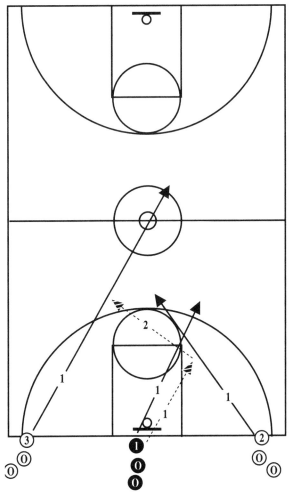

Procedure:

- Players arrange themselves into three lines.
- The drill starts with three basketballs located in the middle line.
- The rule to remember is to pass the ball and go **behind** the receiver.
- O1 passes the ball to O2, then goes behind O2.
- O2 receives the ball from O1, passes to O3, and goes behind O3.
- O3 receives the ball from O2, then passes to O1. This is repeated to the other end.
- When arriving at the far end, the player attempts a lay-in.
- The shooter turns and sprints back to the starting end as soon as the ball is shot and plays defense against the other two.
- On a made lay-in, the offense must take the ball out of bounds to begin play. If the shot is missed, the offense will immediately take off for a two-against-one.

OPTIONAL: Do not allow dribbling at any time.

180

THREE-TWO UNENDING

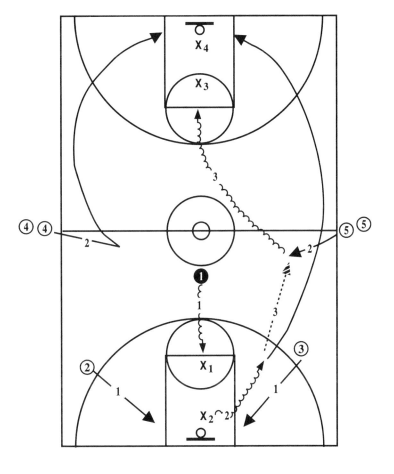

Primary Skill: Offense

Objective: To develop a variety of skills for basketball.

Equipment Needed: One basketball.

Coaching Tips to Players: Concentrate!

Procedure:

- This is a continuous drill.

- O1, O2, and O3 attempt to score against X1 and X2. Play continues until the shot is made or either defender gets the rebound. At this time, two of the three offensive members stay and become the next defenders. The other offensive player goes to line O4 or O5.

- The defender who does not snag the rebound proceeds to the O4 or O5 line.

- The defender who snares the rebound, gives the ball to either O4 or O5, follows the pass, then sprints wide to the other end of the floor to challenge X3 and X4.

- O4 and O5 move toward the ball. The athlete on the rebound side, for example O5, will yell "outlet". After receiving the outlet pass, O5 dribbles to the foul line at the other end and is part of a three-against-two. O4 fills the open lane.

OPTIONAL: Do not allow any dribbling.

181

THREE-TWO, TWO-ONE UNENDING

Primary Skill: Offense

Objective: To develop team play for the open shot, defense, and passing.

Equipment Needed: One basketball.

Coaching Tips to Players: Work together and talk.

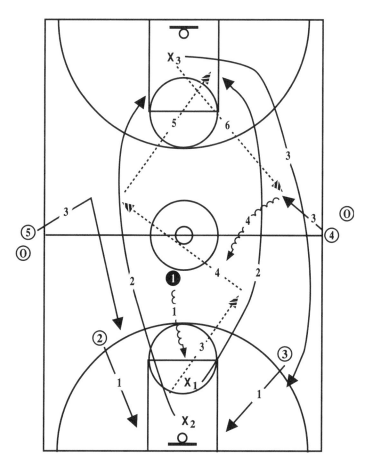

Procedure:

- This is a continuous activity.

- O1, O2, and O3 challenge X1 and X2. Play until a basket is made or the defense nabs the rebound. Two of the offensive players stay to play defense and the other seeks out the shortest O4 or O5 line.

- X1 and X2 retrieve the rebound, on the made or missed shot, and proceed to the other end by passing only. They next attempt to score against the solitary X3. After the shot is made or missed, either X1 or X2 will stay and play defense again while the other player pursues the shortest O4 or O5 line.

- X3 gets the made or missed shot, gives the ball to either O4 or O5. Next X3, O4, and O5 continue down court for a three-against-two at the other end.

- O4 and O5 break toward the single defender to receive the outlet pass. The receiver dribbles down the middle of the court while the other two fill the outside lanes.

TIME MANAGEMENT

Primary Skill: Offense or defense

Objective: To develop the ability to make good decisions when time is running down.

Equipment Needed: One basketball and stop watch.

Coaching Tips to Players: Practicing the various pressure situations that may occur during a game can pay off during a game.

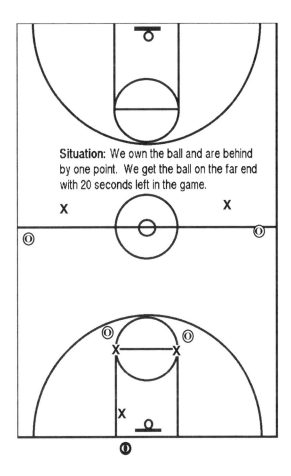

Situation: We own the ball and are behind by one point. We get the ball on the far end with 20 seconds left in the game.

Procedure:

- Divide the team into two units.
- Create a game situation, discuss the goals, strategies, and desired outcomes.
- Place the players in the desired situation and act out the scenario.
- Circumstance indicators might include:
    a. Which team has possession of the ball? *Offense or defense.*
    b. Which team is ahead? *We or they.*
    c. By how much is this team ahead? *Tied, one, two, three.*
    d. Where does play begin? *Under the near basket, under the far basket, at half court, on the side line, on the floor near the three-point line, on the floor at half court, on the floor at the foul line, etc.*
    e. How much time is remaining? *Minutes, seconds.*

OPTIONAL: If a desired outcome is attained, the team that allowed it will run sprints.

TWO-ONE

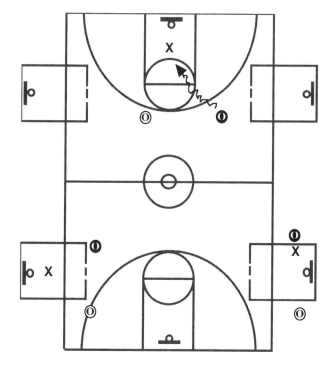

Primary Skill: Offense

Objective: To develop the ability to find the open player.

Equipment Needed: One ball for each group.

Coaching Tips to Players: The offense should stay spread out.

Procedure:

- Players form units of three.
- Each group needs one basketball.
- Play is conducted on a half-court floor.
- Two offensive players will attempt to score.
- One defensive player tries to stop them.
- When either offensive player snares the rebound of a missed shot, play continues.
- The defensive player may rotate out of the key after
  a. Preventing a score.
  b. Playing defense a set number of times.
  c. Creating a turnover.

OPTIONAL: When either offensive player snares the rebound of a missed shot, the ball is brought back out to the extended free-throw line and play continues.

"V" CUTS

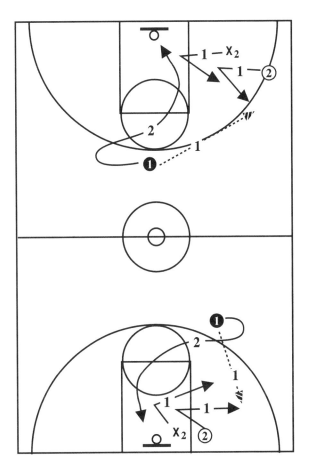

Primary Skill: Offense

Objective: To allow an offensive player to get clear to receive a pass.

Equipment Needed: One ball for each group.

Coaching Tips to Players: Fake hard, as if going to the basket, then break rapidly away.

Procedure:

- Construct groups of three players.
- Each group will need a basketball.
- Disperse the teams to the various baskets.
- O1 passes the ball to O2 and sprints toward the basket for the return pass. Instead of shooting, O1 will dribble to a new location and wait for O2 to "V" cut again.
- O2 makes a "V" cut, receives the ball from O1, then passes the ball back to O1.
- The X2 will put light pressure on O2 when first learning the technique.
- Turn up the defensive pressure as play progresses.
- Rotate positions frequently.

OPTIONAL: Add an extra defender.

OPTIONAL: Allow the offensive team to score after a predetermined number of "V" cuts have been successfully completed.

"V" CUTS CONTINUOUS

Primary Skill: Offense

Objective: To allow an offensive player to get clear to receive a pass.

Equipment Needed: One ball for each group.

Coaching Tips to Players:
Fake hard, as if going to the basket, then break rapidly away.

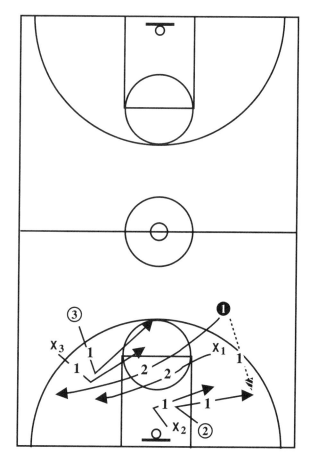

Procedure:

- Players divide into groups of six.
- The object is to make a predetermined number of passes without the defense intercepting or deflecting the ball. Scoring is not allowed.
- O1 passes the ball to an open O2 or O3, then "V" cuts to an open area.
- O2 and O3 make "V" cuts and possibly receive the ball from O1.
- Play is continuous with players performing "V" cuts to get open.
- The defense puts pressure on the offense and tries to prevent the pass.
- The offense always retains possession of the ball, even when errors occur.
- Players rotate from offense to defense after a set amount of time or after a desired number of passes are attained.

OPTIONAL: Divide into groups of four.

OPTIONAL: After a predetermined number of passes, the offense will attempt to score.

Section 9

PASSING

Success covers a multitude of blunders.

—George Bernard Shaw

AIRMAIL

Primary Skill: Passing

Objective: To pass the ball accurately over a long distance.

Equipment Needed: One ball.

Coaching Tips to Players: Watch out for the backboard being in the way and lead the runner with the pass.

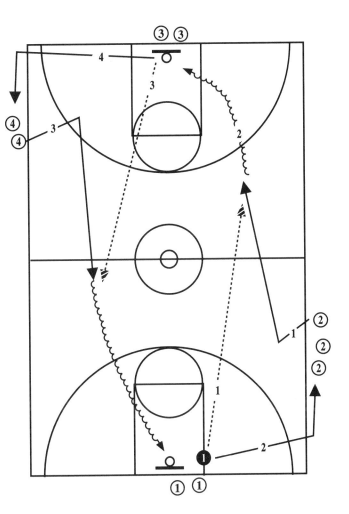

Procedure:

- Only one basketball is needed for this continuous drill.
- Players must grab the rebound, quickly step out of bounds, and then throw the pass.
- O1 passes to O2 and proceeds to O2's location.
- O2 receives a pass from O1, dribbles in for the score, then remains at O3's site.
- O3 grabs O2's rebound, passes the ball to O4, then advances to O4's spot.
- O4 receives a pass from O3, dribbles down for the lay-in, and stays at O1's area.
- Use a variety of passes such as the baseball pass, hook pass, long skip pass, or the bowling pass. The bowling pass is rolled rapidly on the floor.
- After a predetermined amount of time, change the lines so that lay-ins are made from the left side.

OPTIONAL: Use two basketballs and start one at each end.

OPTIONAL: Players may elect to shoot any shot.

AROUND THE HORN

Primary Skill: Passing

Objective: To develop accurate passing.

Equipment Needed: Two basketballs.

Coaching Tips to Players: While stepping forward with the body, also push with the arms and wrists.

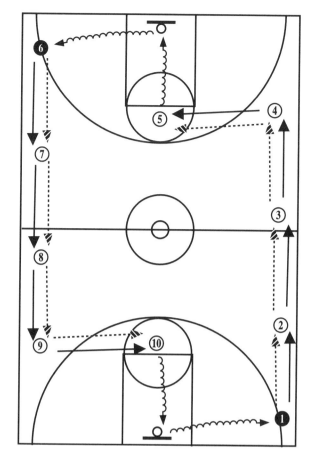

Procedure:

- Players disperse around the court as shown in the above illustration.
- Play starts with two basketballs at opposite ends of the court.
- Players pass the ball and move up one position.
- Play is continuous.
- O1 passes to O2, then assumes O2's location.
- At the same time O1 passes, O6 passes to O7, then assumes O7's spot.
- O2 receives the pass from O1, passes to O3, and advances.
- O5 receives the pass from O4, dribbles for a lay-in, rebounds, dribbles to the corner, and passes to O6.
- The ball is passed around using various passes. Including the two-handed chest pass, the one-hand push, the bounce, the two-hand overhead, the wrap around, the touch pass, the lob, and the behind-the-back pass.

BANDIT

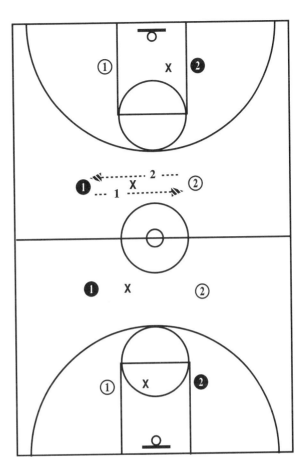

Primary Skill: Passing

Objective: To develop passing skills against a defender.

Equipment Needed: One ball for every three players.

Coaching Tips to Players:
Make good fakes and quick passes.

Procedure:

- Players break into several groups of three.

- One basketball is needed for each group.

- O1 and O2 are about ten feet apart and play catch. They are allowed only one step prior to passing or catching the ball.

- The ball is passed around using various passes including the chest pass, the one-hand push pass, the bounce pass, the overhead pass, the wrap-around pass, the touch pass, and the behind-the-back pass.

- Passes may not be thrown higher than the extended arms of the defender.

- The defender may not drop back more than half the distance between O1 and O2. The defender tries to intercept or deflect the ball. If successful, the defender changes positions with the player who threw the bad pass.

OPTIONAL: Neither O1 nor O2 may throw the same pass two times in a row.

BLIND CATCH

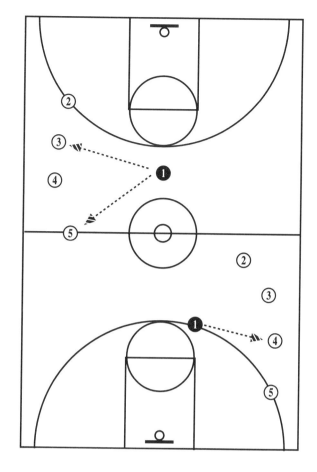

Primary Skill: Passing

Objective: To develop quick reactions when catching the ball.

Equipment Needed: One ball per group.

Coaching Tips to Players: Keep the hands above the waist.

Diagram Notes: Upper court illustrates two balls being tossed simultaneously

Procedure:

- The team divides into two units.
- Each group needs one basketball.
- Passers should be at least 15 feet away from the line of receivers.
- O1 throws the ball to any of the players. As soon as the ball leaves O1's hands, O1 yells, "Now".
- O2, O3, O4, and O5 stand motionless, facing away from the ball, and have both hands poised and ready. The hands should be held near the middle of the chest with the elbows about waist high.
- When O2 through O5 hear O1 shout, they will instantly turn around, look for a ball coming directly at them, and if so, catch it.
- Players rotate one position clockwise after every five passes.

OPTIONAL: O1 will toss two balls at the same time to different players.

BULL IN THE RING

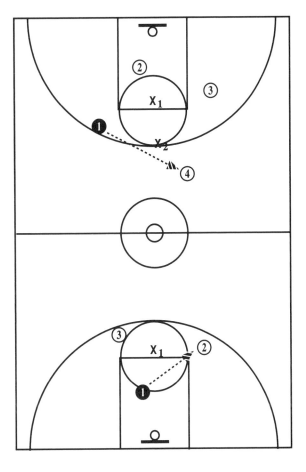

Primary Skill: Passing

Objective: To develop passing skill against a defender.

Equipment Needed: One ball for every four players.

Coaching Tips to Players: Make good fakes and quick passes.

Diagram Notes: Upper court illustrates the use of more players in the middle and on the outside.

Procedure:

- Players form groups of four.
- Each group requires one basketball.
- Use either the free-throw circle or the center jump circle.
- O1, O2, and O3 must always be touching the circle with one foot while playing keep-away from X1.
- The defender tries to intercept or deflect the ball. When the defender is successful, X1 immediately changes positions with the player who threw the bad pass.
- Passes may not be thrown higher than the extended arms of the defender.

OPTIONAL: Increase the distance between the participants.

OPTIONAL: Do not allow the passer to fake any passes.

OPTIONAL: Place two defenders in the middle and four or five others around the ring.

OPTIONAL: Use two basketballs with the above option.

ERASURE

Primary Skill: Passing

Objective: To increase passing proficiency

Equipment Needed: One ball.

Coaching Tips to Players:
Pass, then move, and when on defense, stay in the passing lane.

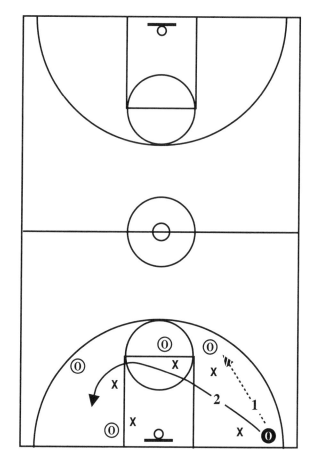

Procedure:

- Players make two teams and play inside the three-point line.

- Dribbling is not allowed.

- A player may hold the ball for only three seconds.

- The goal for either team is to get to a predetermined number of passes. Each completed pass is worth one point.

- When the defense either deflects the ball, steals a pass, or forces the offense to throw the ball away, they gain possession and begin reducing the other team's score or adding to their own. Example: Team "A": 1, 2, 3, 4, 5, Team "B" steals: -4, -3, -2; -1, 1, 2, Team "A" deflects: -1, 1, 2, 3, 4, 5, 6, 7, 8, 9, 10, 11, 12, Team "B" forces a pass out of bounds: -11, -10; Team "A" touches the ball: 11, 12, and so on.

OPTIONAL: Reduce the size of the playing area.

OPTIONAL: Reduce the number of players on each team.

FAST ATTACK

Primary Skill: Passing

Objective: To quickly get the ball into play after a made basket.

Equipment Needed: Two basketballs.

Coaching Tips to Players: Grab the rebound as soon as possible.

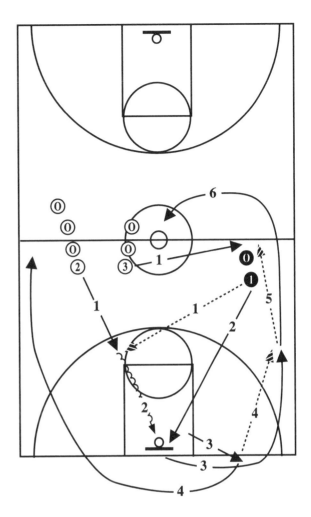

Procedure:

- Players form three lines near middle court.
- Two basketballs will be needed.
- O1 reverse pivots and passes the ball to O2. O1 then retrieves the rebound, sprints out of bounds with the ball and outlets the ball to O2. O1 next goes to the shooting line via the outside.
- O2 breaks to the basket, receives the pass from O1, dribbles in for the shot, sprints out to the far side, receives the outlet pass from O1, passes the ball to O3, then goes to the end of the receiving line.
- O3 breaks to the outlet line as soon as O2 receives the pass from O1, then proceeds to the passing line.

NOTE: This can be a great warm-up drill.

OPTIONAL: O2 may choose any shot desired.

195

FIVE-PERSON WEAVE

Primary Skill: Passing

Objective: To develop teamwork.

Equipment Needed: One basketball for each group.

Coaching Tips to Players:
Make good crisp passes.

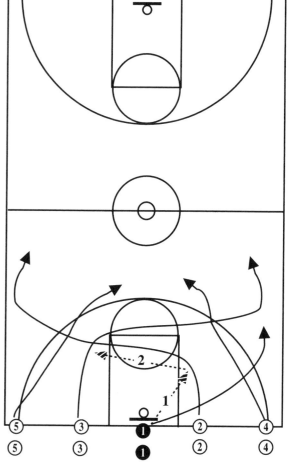

Procedure:

- Players divide into five lines.
- Locate at one end of the court.
- Start with the two basketballs located in the middle line.
- The rule to remember is to pass the ball and go **behind** two players.
- The entire unit will go down and back, attempting to make a lay-in at both ends.
- Dribbling is not allowed.
- O1 passes the ball to O2, then cuts behind both O2 and O4.
- O2 receives the pass, moves down court, passes the ball to O3, then cuts behind both O3 and O5.
- O4 and O5 move down court, angle in toward the center, and wait for a pass.

OPTIONAL: Do not five-person weave coming back. Come back along the side lines. The second group will go as soon at the first is at half court.

FLIP FLOP

Primary Skill: Passing

Objective: To develop passing accuracy.

Equipment Needed: One basketball.

Coaching Tips to Players: Make a crisp pass.

Diagram Notes: Upper court illustrates the use of two basketballs for more passing opportunities.

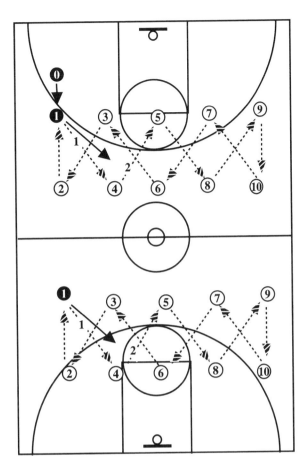

Procedure:

- Players form two lines.
- Only one basketball is needed.
- Players will always follow their pass.
- O1 passes to O4 and quickly assumes the spot of a vacating O4.
- O4 passes to O5 and quickly assumes the spot of a vacating O5.
- O5 passes to O8 and so on.
- Play is never ending.
- Passes should include the chest pass, the one-hand push pass, the bounce pass, the overhead pass, and the behind-the-back pass.

OPTIONAL: Do not follow the ball after passing it.

OPTIONAL: Use two basketballs. One extra player will be stationed behind O1 at the beginning of the drill.

FOUR CORNERS

Primary Skill: Passing

Objective: To develop the skill of passing to a moving target.

Equipment Needed: One or two balls.

Coaching Tips to Players: Throw the pass in front of the moving player.

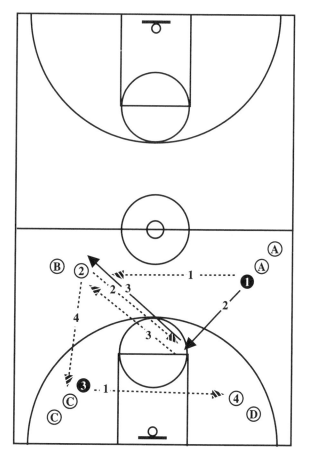

Procedure:

- Players form four lines near the corners of a half-court playing area.

- Two basketballs will be needed. They will be located opposite each other.

NOTE: For ease of explanation, only the tasks of O1 and O2 are described here. O3 and O4 simultaneously perform the same routine.

- O1 passes the basketball to O2, sprints to the middle of the square, and receives the return pass from O2

- O1 fires the ball back to O2, then advances to end of line "B".

- After receiving the second pass from O1, O2 passes the ball to the second person in line "C", sprints to the middle, and waits for the return pass. Play is continuous.

- Stress that players on opposite side are to stay synchronized.

NOTE: This drill makes an excellent warm-up drill.

HOT POTATO

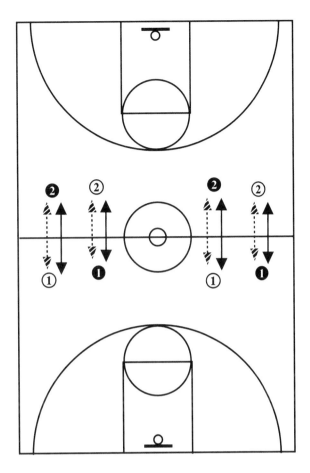

Primary Skill: Passing

Objective: To develop ball control when catching and passing rapidly.

Equipment Needed: One ball for every two players.

Coaching Tips to Players:
Catch the ball first, then pass it back.

Procedure:

- Players pick a partner.
- Each pair needs one basketball.
- O1 and O2 stand about five feet apart.
- Begin passing the ball rapidly back and forth, all the while, moving slowly backwards.
- When approximately 15 feet apart, slowly return to the five-foot distance.
- Repeat the above routine using the following passes:
  a. Two-hand chest
  b. One-hand push
  c. Bounce
  d. Over the head
  e. Touch

OPTIONAL: Make groups of three or four players but use only one ball.

199

KEEP AWAY

Primary Skill: Passing

Objective: To develop passing skills.

Equipment Needed: One basketball.

Coaching Tips to Players: Keep moving, set screens, and communicate.

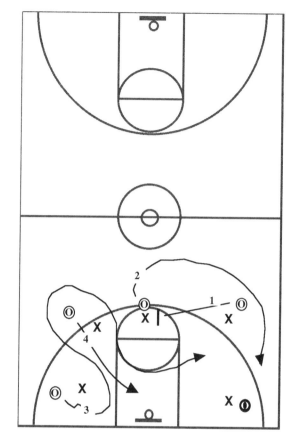

Procedure:

- The team divides into units of five.
- The drill requires a half-court setting and one basketball.
- Play a game in which a predetermined number of passes needs to be completed without a mistake. If this is accomplished, the offense and defense switch.
- The offense must start over whenever the defense
    a. Touches the ball.
    b. Intercepts a pass.
    c. Forces an errant pass.
    d. Causes steps to be taken.
- Switch whenever the offense is successful or the defense creates a fifth restart.

OPTIONAL: Players may not throw the same type of a pass two times in a row.

OPTIONAL: Remove the air from the ball so that dribbling is next to impossible.

MACHINE GUN

Primary Skill: Passing

Objective: To develop concentration when passing.

Equipment Needed: Two balls for each group.

Coaching Tips to Players: Use your peripheral vision.

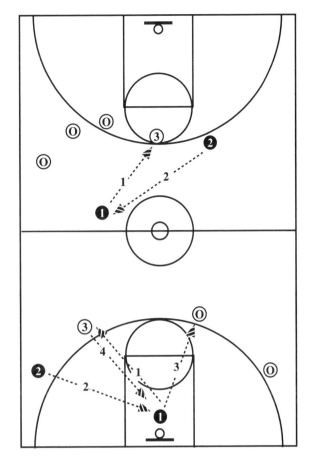

Procedure:

- The team divides in half.
- O1 and O2 each have a basketball.
- O1 passes a ball to each of the other players.
- The passes are thrown to each player in sequential order.
- As soon as O1 passes the ball to O3, O2 passes the ball to O1.
- As soon as O1 passes the ball to O4, O3 passes the ball to O1 and so on.
- Each player quickly returns the ball to O1. This pass must be thrown a split second **after** O1 has passed the ball.
- Players rotate one position clockwise after the ball has been passed down the line and back twice.

OPTIONAL: O1 can pass to any player at anytime.

OPTIONAL: Use one basketball and some other type of a ball.

MARCH MADNESS

Primary Skill: Passing

Objective: To develop passing accuracy.

Equipment Needed: Two basketballs.

Coaching Tips to Players: Focus on a target.

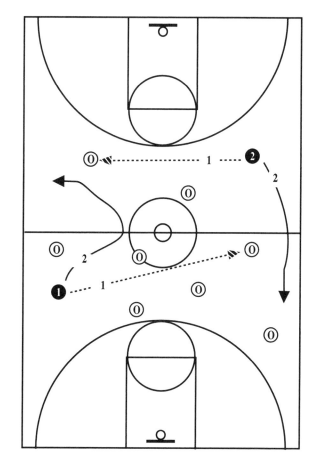

Procedure:

- Players disperse between the three-point shooting lines.
- Two basketballs are needed.
- O1 and O2 pass the ball to any other player, then assume a new location that is more than 15 feet away.
- Players are not allowed to possess a ball for more than three seconds.
- Dribbling is not allowed.
- Play is continuous.

OPTIONAL: Add three or four basketballs.

OPTIONAL: Use the entire floor.

OPTIONAL: Add different types of balls.

OPTIONAL: Allow moving players to deflect or intercept passes. If a player's pass is intercepted, they will go to a specific area and perform a stunt before returning.

MIRROR IMAGE

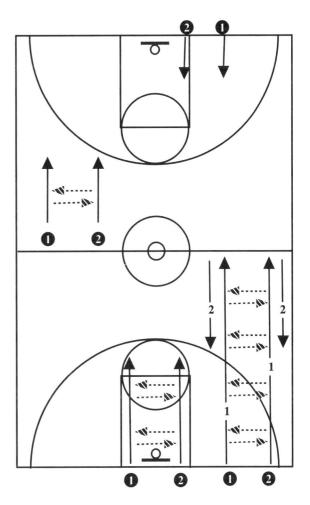

Primary Skill: Passing

Objective: To develop hand and eye coordination.

Equipment Needed: One basketball for each player.

Coaching Tips to Players: Stay focused.

Procedure:

- Players pair up with a teammate.
- Each player has a basketball.
- O1 and O2 always face each other.
- Participants must maintain a six-foot buffer zone.
- While side sliding to half court and back, O1 and O2 pass and catch both basketballs simultaneously.
- Attempt these stunts:
   a. Pass from the right hand to the partner's left hand.
   b. Pass from the left hand to the partner's right hand.
   c. Use the bounce pass and repeat the above two stunts.
   d. O1 passes through the air, while O2 uses the bounce pass.

OPTIONAL: *Use a heavy trainer.*

MIRROR MIRROR

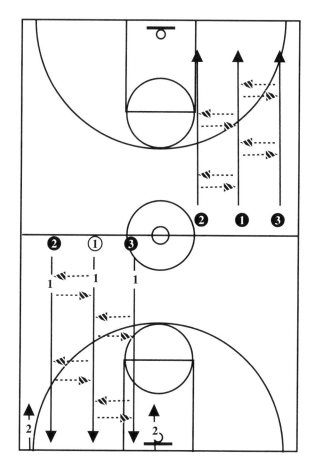

Primary Skill: Passing

Objective: To develop hand and eye coordination.

Equipment Needed: Two basketballs for each threesome.

Coaching Tips to Players: Stay focused.

Diagram Notes: Upper court depicts the use of three basketballs for more difficulty.

Procedure:

- Players form groups of threes.
- Each player on the outside of O1 has a basketball.
- Participants must maintain a six-foot buffer zone while side sliding.
- O2 and O3 always face each other.
- While sliding to half court and back, O2 and O3 pass and catch their ball with O1.
- O1 alternates passes between O2 and O3. To face the opposite player after each pass, O1 should use the reverse pivot.
- Use various types of passes. These should include the chest pass, the one-hand push pass, the bounce pass, the overhead pass, and the touch pass.
- The players should rotate lines after each down and back.

OPTIONAL: Use a heavy trainer.

OPTIONAL: Use three basketballs.

NO DRIBBLE

Primary Skill: Passing

Objective: To develop passing skills.

Equipment Needed: One basketball.

Coaching Tips to Players: Pass and cut through the middle.

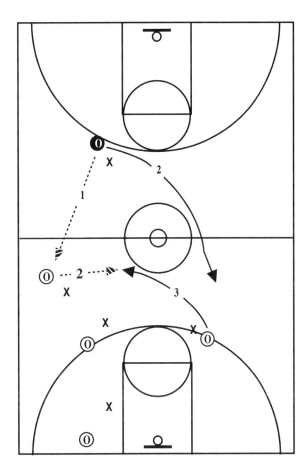

Procedure:

- Play a game of basketball in which dribbling is not allowed.
- This game can be played in either half or full court.
- Practice all of the different types of passes.
  - a. Chest
  - b. One-hand push
  - c. Bounce
  - d. Over the head
  - e. Behind the back
  - f. Wrap around
  - g. Touch
  - h. Lob

OPTIONAL: Remove the air from the ball so that it is very difficult to dribble the ball.

PASS PASS PASS

Primary Skill: Passing

Objective: To develop skill in passing to a moving player.

Equipment Needed: One ball for each group.

Coaching Tips to Players: Pass the ball slightly in front of the moving player.

Diagram Notes: Upper court illustrates a different formation.

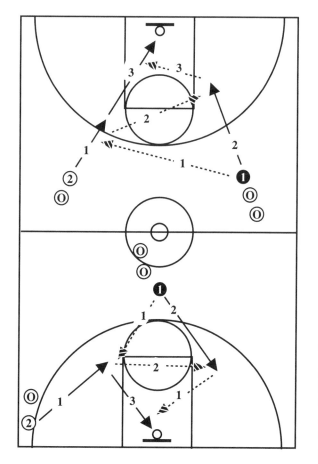

Procedure:

- O1 passes the ball to a moving O2.
- O2 breaks toward the rim and receives a pass from O1, then stops.
- O1 breaks toward the basket and gets the return pass from O2.
- O2 breaks to the basket and gets the final pass from O1 for a lay-in.
- Players should switch lines each time through.
- Practice all of the different types of passes:
  - a. Chest
  - b. One-hand push
  - c. Bounce
  - d. Over the head
  - e. Behind the back
  - f. Touch

PASSING RELAY

Primary Skill: Passing

Objective: To improve the speed and accuracy of the various kinds of passes.

Equipment Needed: One ball for each line.

Coaching Tips to Players: Step with the body; push with the arms and wrists.

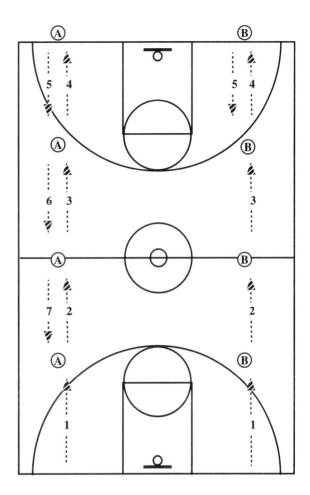

Procedure:

- Players make two or three equal teams, then form a straight line on the floor.

- The object is to be the first team to pass the ball down and back three times.

- Players must catch the ball and not just push it on by. After the catch, players pivot and pass to the next person, unless stationed on either end.

- If a pass goes astray, the receiver must return to his or her spot before passing it again.

- Players rotate positions with the start of each new contest.

- Use the various types of passes such as

  a. Two-hand chest pass

  b. Bounce or skip

  c. Over the head

  d. One-hand push (right and left)

  e. Behind the back

RAPID FIRE

Primary Skill: Passing

Objective: To develop passing skills.

Equipment Needed: One basketball for each group.

Coaching Tips to Players: Make sure to use the wrists.

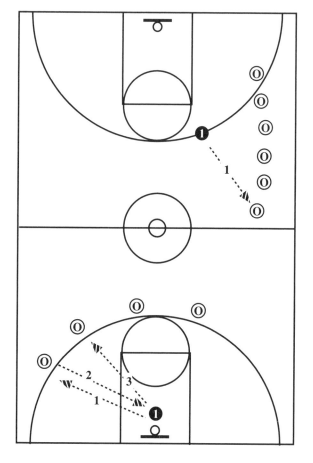

Procedure:

- O1 quickly passes the ball to each player in sequence.
- Each player quickly return passes it back to O1.
- Players rotate positions after the ball has been passed down the line and back twice.
- Practice all of the different types of passes:
    a. Chest
    b. One-hand push
    c. Bounce
    d. Over the head
    e. Behind the back
    f. Wrap around
    g. Touch

OPTIONAL: O1 may pass to any player at any time.

RUSH

Primary Skill: Passing

Objective: To quickly move the ball to the other end of the court.

Equipment Needed: One basketball.

Coaching Tips to Players: Lead the runner when passing the ball.

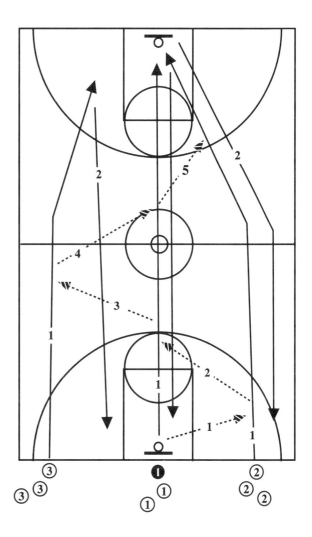

Procedure:

- Players form three lines at the end of the basketball court.
- Only one basketball is needed.
- Players stay in the same lane when moving down the floor and back.
- Dribbling is not allowed.
- O1 alternates passes with O2 and O3 while running down the court. O1 retrieves the rebound on the shot attempt, then passes to O2 or O3 as soon as possible.
- The wing that does not shoot the ball at the other end turns and sprints in the opposite direction, all the while looking for the return pass from either O1 or O2. Once the ball has been caught, the wing attempts to score a lay-in.
- O1 or O2 long distance passes the ball to O3 at the earliest opportunity.
- All players should switch lines each time back.

OPTIONAL: Players must go again if either lay-in is missed.

SEE NO EVIL

Primary Skill: Passing

Objective: To look one way and pass another.

Equipment Needed: Two basketballs.

Coaching Tips to Players: Use peripheral vision.

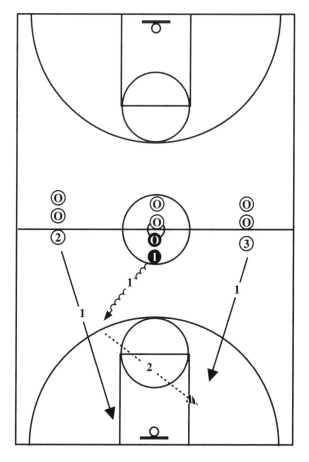

Procedure:

- Players form three lines at center court.
- Passers are never to look directly at the teammate who is to receive the ball, even when passing the ball back to the center line.
- O1 dribbles to the key, looks one way, then passes the ball to either O2 or O3.
- O2 and O3 break to the basket in anticipation of the ball.
- Switch lines each session.
- Use the various types of passes.

OPTIONAL: The coach will stand under the basket and point to where the ball is to be passed. The dribbler must always look at the coach's hand.

OPTIONAL: Make two units and go in opposite directions from half court.

OPTIONAL: Add one or two defenders in the key. Require a predetermined number of passes before a shot may be attempted.

SHOVE BACK

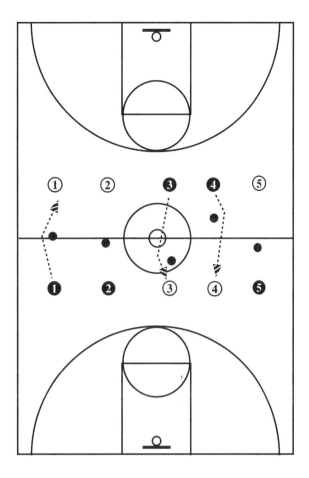

Primary Skill: Passing

Objective: To develop accurate passing skills.

Equipment Needed: One ball and one coin, poker chip, or plastic lid for each pair.

Coaching Tips to Players: Focus on the object in the middle.

Procedure:

- Each player picks a partner.
- Each pair will need one basketball.
- Partners stand about 15 to 20 feet apart.
- A line on the floor should be directly in between them.
- Set the coin or lid on the line.
- Participants can use only a two-handed chest pass.
- Players pass the basketball back and forth, attempting to move the object into the opponent's territory.
- A winner is declared after a predetermined amount of time has expired.

OPTIONAL: Increase the distance between the players.

OPTIONAL: Allow each player only ten passes to determine the winner.

OPTIONAL: Change the type of pass that may be used.

SLIDE AND PASS

Primary Skill: Passing

Objective: To develop skills for passing to a moving player.

Equipment Needed: One basketball for every two lines.

Coaching Tips to Players: Lead the player slightly.

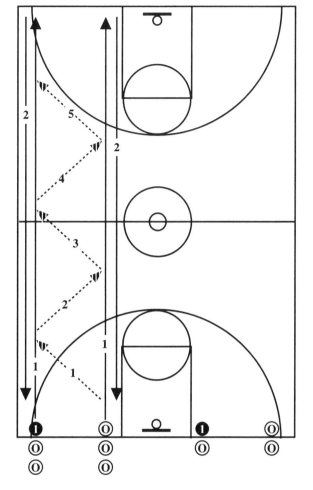

Procedure:

- O1 and O2 pass the ball back and forth while side sliding down and back the full length of the court.

- Use these various types of passes:
  a. Chest
  b. Above the head
  c. Bounce
  d. One hand push
  e. Touch

OPTIONAL: Use a basketball that has had weight added to it. They are known as medicine balls or heavy trainers.

OPTIONAL: Use any type of a ball other than a basketball—a beach ball, soccer ball, tennis ball, or football.

STAR CHAMBER

Primary Skill: Passing

Objective: To develop passing and concentration.

Equipment Needed: One or two balls for each group of players.

Coaching Tips to Players: Stay focused.

Diagram Notes: Upper court illustrates the drill with the use of two basketballs.

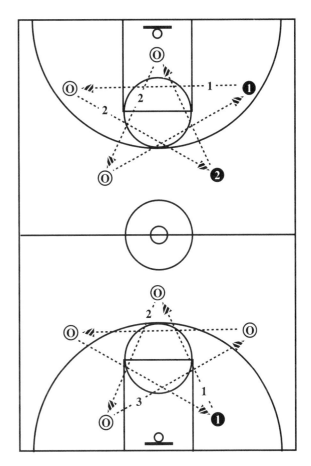

Procedure:

- Five players will form the points of a star.
- O1 passes the ball to the second player to the right.
- The receiver catches the ball and also passes it to the second player to the right.
- Play is continuous.
- Practice all of the different types of passes:
  a. Chest
  b. One-hand push
  c. Bounce
  d. Over the head
  e. Behind the back

OPTIONAL: Change the direction of the ball when a whistle is blown.

OPTIONAL: Use two basketballs.

SUPER NOVA

Primary Skill: Passing

Objective: To develop passing in a synchronized manner.

Equipment Needed: Four balls.

Coaching Tips to Players: Attempt to arrive at the center at the same time.

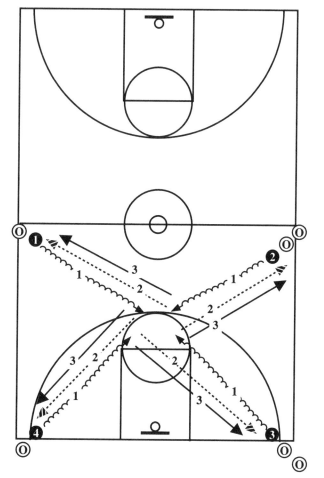

Procedure:

- Players form four lines at the corners of a half court.
- Each line starts with a basketball.
- This drill is continuous.
- The objective is to have all four players mirroring each other.
- O1, O2, O3, and O4 have a ball and simultaneously dribble to the center. Next, all four jump stop, reverse pivot, pass the ball outward to the next line, then proceed to the end of that line.
- The next person in line receives the pass and does the same as the previous participants.

OPTIONAL: The various types of passes, chest, bounce, behind the back, etc., can be used.

OPTIONAL: Players may reverse pivot and pass back to the line they originally came from. The ball is subsequently passed back to the middle, then forwarded to the next line.

THREE-ON-THREE NO DRIBBLE

Primary Skill: Passing

Objective: To develop controlled passing.

Equipment Needed: One ball for each group of six players.

Coaching Tips to Players: Pass and move.

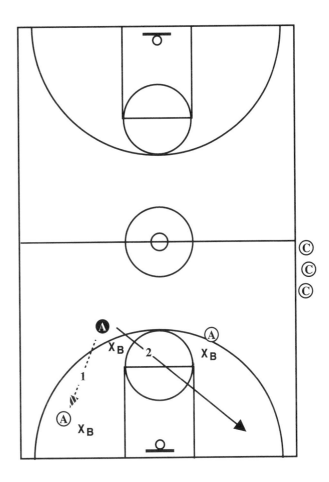

Procedure:

- Players divide into three equal teams.
- This is a half-court game.
- All of the rules of basketball apply except that dribbling is not allowed.
- The ball is passed around using the various passes. These should include the chest pass, the one-hand push pass, the bounce pass, the overhead pass, the wrap-around pass, the touch pass, and the behind-the-back pass.
- First team to score five baskets is declared the winner.
- Winners will stay and take on the new group of challengers.

OPTIONAL: Require a specific number of passes to be thrown before a shot can be taken.

OPTIONAL: Take the air out of the ball.

OPTIONAL: Use a different type of ball—a volleyball, beach ball, etc.

OPTIONAL: Use the full court.

THREE-PERSON WEAVE

Primary Skill: Conditioning

Objective: To develop team-work and ball control.

Equipment Needed: One basketball for every three players.

Coaching Tips to Players: Stay focused and alert.

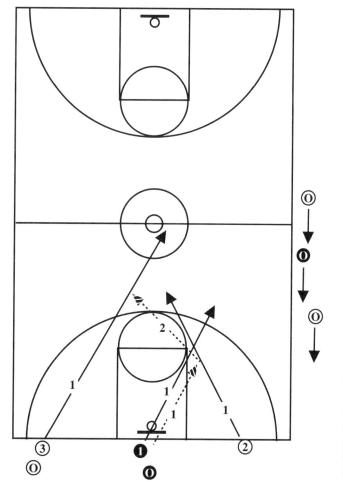

Procedure:

- Players divide into three lines and locate at one end of the court.
- Play starts with the three basketballs in the middle line.
- The rule to remember is to pass the ball and go **behind** the receiver.
- O1 passes the ball to O2, then goes behind O2.
- O2 receives the ball from O1, passes to O3, and goes behind O3.
- O3 receives the ball from O2, then passes to O1.
- This is repeated to the other end.
- When arriving at the far end, the player attempts a lay-in.
- The player returns with the ball via the sidelines.
- As soon as a group has reached half court, the next unit begins.

OPTIONAL: Return to the start by playing a two-against-one. The shooter is the defender.

TOUCH-ME-NOT

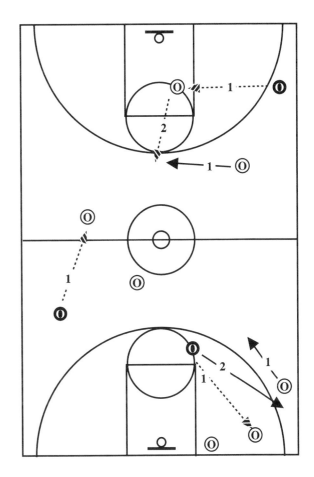

Primary Skill: Passing

Objective: To quickly and accurately pass the ball without catching it first.

Equipment Needed: One basketball for each group.

Coaching Tips to Players: Lead the player if s/he is moving.

Diagram Notes: Court illustrations show different types of movement.

Procedure:

- Players form groups of three or four.
- Players in each group maintain a distance of 10 to 15 feet apart.
- The ball is passed around using the various passes. These should include the chest pass, the one-hand push pass, the bounce pass, the overhead pass, the wrap-around pass, and the behind-the-back pass.
- From time to time, players will touch-pass the ball to a teammate.
- The basketball may be directly touch-passed back to the sender.
- Players may move about freely.

OPTIONAL: Use a beach ball.

OPTIONAL: Use a volleyball.

OPTIONAL: Every third pass must be a touch-pass.

OPTIONAL: See how many times the ball can be touch-passed without it hitting the floor.

TOUCH-N-GO

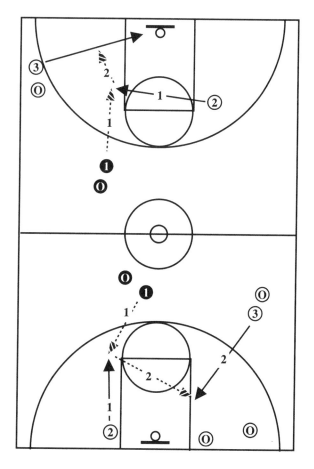

Primary Skill: Passing

Objective: To be able to pass the ball without holding on to it.

Equipment Needed: Two basketballs for each group.

Coaching Tips to Players:
Lead the player with the pass when s/he is moving.

Diagram Notes: Court illustrations show different types of movement.

Procedure:

- The team breaks into two units and goes to opposite ends of the court with one basketball.

- O1 passes the ball to O2.

- O2 receives the pass from O1 and touch-passes the ball to O3.

- O2 will stay in the key area for four or five different touch-passes before rotating out.

- O3 breaks toward the basket and receives the touch-pass from O2. O3 can shoot, dribble, regular pass, or touch-pass the ball back to either O1 or O2.

- O1 and O3 will rotate positions each time they are involved in the drill.

OPTIONAL: Add one defensive player against O2.

OPTIONAL: Add three defenders. Scoring is not allowed. Attempt to pass the ball around and touch-pass the ball as often as possible.

OPTIONAL: Restrict the area and use a beach ball. Add defenders. Scoring is not allowed.

WAGON WHEEL

Primary Skill: Passing

Objective: To develop skill in passing from the dribble and passing to a moving teammate.

Equipment Needed: Two basketballs.

Coaching Tips to Players: Use peripheral vision.

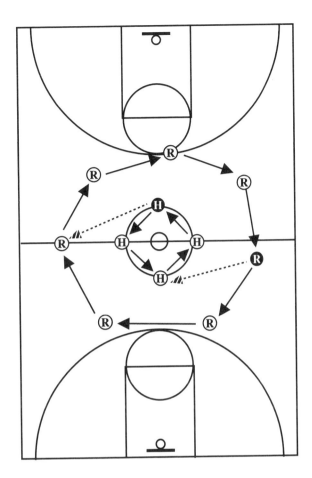

Procedure:

- Players form the rim and the hub of the wheel. They always rotate in opposite directions.
- The spokes are created by passing the balls back and forth from the hub to the rim.
- When in possession of the ball, players may dribble. They may stop and pivot or pass on the move to anyone who is facing them.
- On the sound of the whistle, the hub and rim reverse directions.
- Use the various types of passes such as
    a. Chest
    b. Touch
    c. Bounce
    d. Over the head
    e. Behind the back

OPTIONAL: Change the speed by calling out, "walk", "jog", "sprint", "run", or "stop".

WALL PASSES

Primary Skill: Passing

Objective: To develop proper passing form and technique.

Equipment Needed: One ball for each player.

Coaching Tips to Players: Step with the body, push with the arm, snap with the wrists.

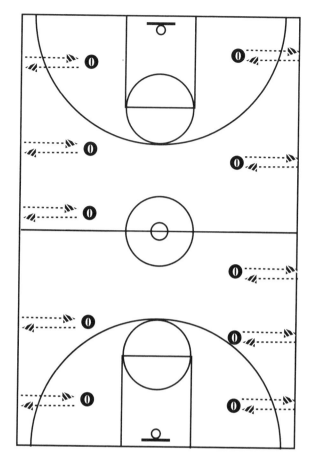

Procedure:

- Each player will need one basketball.
- Players will stand 10 feet away from the wall.
- Practice all of the different types of passes such as:
    a. Chest
    b. One-hand push
    c. Bounce
    d. Over the head
    e. Wrap around
    f. Behind the back

OPTIONAL: Increase or decrease the distance.

OPTIONAL: Use a heavy trainer.

OPTIONAL: How many times can the wall be hit in 30 seconds?

WALL TARGETS

Primary Skill: Passing

Objective: To develop proper pass-ing form and accuracy.

Equipment Needed: One ball for each player; masking tape targets on the wall.

Coaching Tips to Players:
Focus on the target.

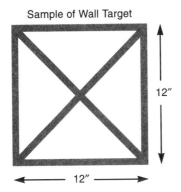

Sample of Wall Target

12″

12″

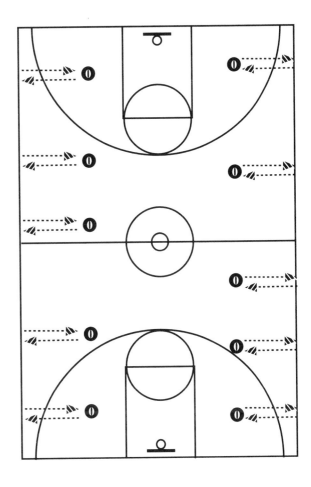

Procedure:

- Players will stand 10 to 15 feet away from the wall. Distance can be increased as accu-racy improves.

- The object is to try to hit the wall target.

- Practice all of the different types of passes such as

    a. Chest

    b. One-hand push

    c. Bounce

    d. Over the head

    e. Wrap around

    f. Behind the back

OPTIONAL: How many times can the target be hit in a given amount of time or number of attempts?

OPTIONAL: How many times can the target be hit in a row?

WORK UP

Primary Skill: Passing

Objective: To develop passing accuracy to a moving player.

Equipment Needed: One basketball.

Coaching Tips to Players: Lead the runner with the ball

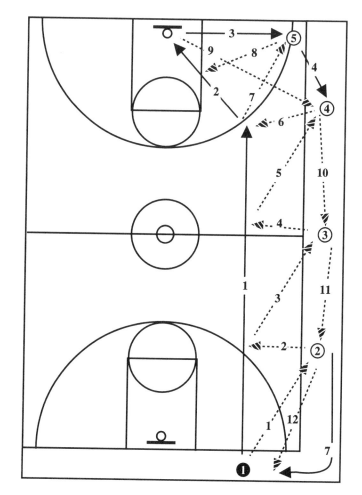

Procedure:

- Any number of players can be on the side of the court.

- Dribbling is not allowed.

- While moving toward the other end, O1 passes the ball to O2, receives the pass back from O2, passes the ball O3 and so on. After receiving the ball from O5, O1 will make the lay-in, retrieve the rebound, pass it to O5, and move to O5's last locale.

- After returning the ball to the runner, side line passers will move up one spot.

- Switch directions after a given amount of time so that left handed lay-ins are attempted.

OPTIONAL: Divide the team in half. Set up the drill on both sides so that lay-ins are being made at both ends.

OPTIONAL: Mirror the right and left sides. Lay-ins are at the same end. Players go to the opposite side after shooting.

WORM WEAVE

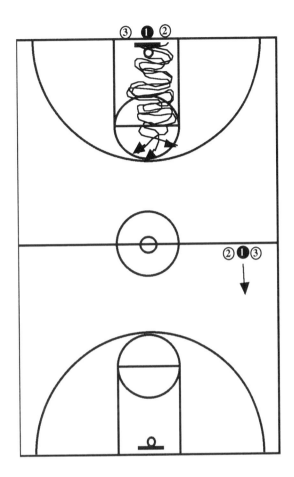

Primary Skill: Passing

Objective: To develop the hand-off pass in tight proximities and for teammates to work together.

Equipment Needed: One basketball for each group.

Coaching Tips to Players:
Present the ball for the easy hand-off.

Procedure:

- This is an extremely tight three-person weave.
- Players divide into groups of three.
- Each group will need one basketball.
- Threesomes spread out at both ends of a basketball court.
- Participants should stand side by side, with the shoulders touching.
- O1 hands the ball to O2, then steps behind O2.
- O2 receives the ball from O1, hands it to O3, then moves behind O3.
- O3 receives the ball from O2, hands it to O1, and so on down the court.
- Advance to half court, stop, turn around, and repeat the drill coming back.

OPTIONAL: Do not use a ball when first learning the tight weave.

OPTIONAL: Perform the same drill using five players. After the hand-off in the middle, the passer must move behind two players each time.

REBOUNDING

*A pessimist sees the difficulty in every opportunity;
an optimist sees the opportunity in every difficulty.*

—Sir Winston Churchill

BACK TO BACK

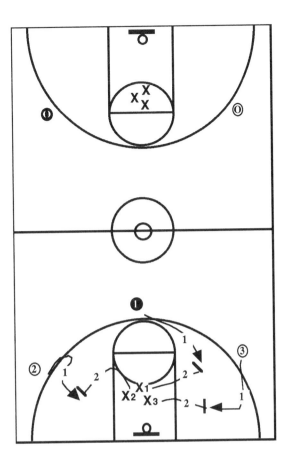

Primary Skill: Rebounding

Objective: To develop skill in blocking out.

Equipment Needed: One basketball for each group.

Coaching Tips to Players: Look for a player to block out first. Go for the rebound second.

Diagram Notes: Upper court dipicts an optional three defenders set.

Procedure:

- Players form groups of three.
- Three offensive players start outside the three-point arc. One of them shoots the ball.
- Three defenders sit in the middle of the key with their backs touching. As soon as the ball is released, all three defenders stand up and find an offensive player to block out.
- Every defender must make contact with an offensive player before going for the ball.
- If the offense attains the rebound, they must get the ball beyond the three-point arc before initiating a scoring attempt.
- Players rotate positions every three sessions.

OPTIONAL: Require defensive players to lie down prior to the shot.

OPTIONAL: Put four in the middle against three on the outside.

OPTIONAL: Put four or five on each side.

BLOCK BUSTER

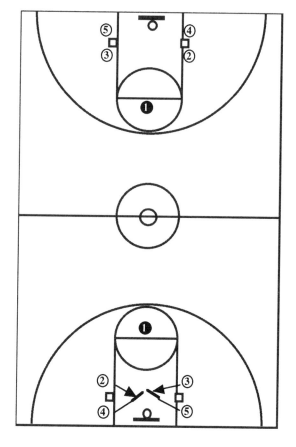

Primary Skill: Rebounding

Objective: To develop skill in rebounding a missed foul shot.

Equipment Needed: One basketball for each group.

Coaching Tips to Players: Fake, spin, or do what is needed to get the ball.

© 1999 by Parker Publishing Company

Procedure:

- Players break into two groups and assemble for a free-throw situation at each end.

- O1 shoots the first foul shot with the good hand. If the shot is made, then all other foul shots by O1 must be with the off hand.

- Any time O2 and O3 get a rebound, they have five seconds to score. When O4 or O5 grab the rebound, O2 and O3 will immediately transform to defense.

- Any time O4 and O5 snare the rebound, they must pass it back to O1, wait to receive the return pass from O1, and then have five seconds in which to try to score.

- This action is repeated until a basket is made.

- All players rotate one position clockwise after a basket has been scored by either O2, O3, O4, or O5. Play continues as before.

OPTIONAL: Play a game to six points. Rotate players when starting a new contest.

BLOCK OUT PIVOTS

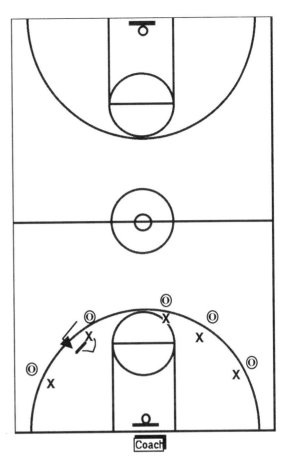

Primary Skill: Rebounds

Objective: To develop skills for preventing the offense from attaining a rebound.

Equipment Needed: Nothing.

Coaching Tips to Players:
Maintain pressure with the body.

Procedure:

- Players pair up and spread out around the three-point arc.
- One player in each pair is on defense, and the other is on offense.
- This is a technique drill. There will be no shooting when first learning the methods.
- On the command of "Shot" all defensive players will practice the following box-out techniques five times and then switch with the partner.
  - a. Reverse pivot to the right into the opponent.
  - b. Reverse pivot to the left.
  - c. Front pivot to the right into the opponent.
  - d. Front pivot to the left.

OPTIONAL: As the coach shoots the ball from various locations, the defenders must practice each one of the four types of block-outs. They can not use the same one twice in a row.

OPTIONAL: If the offense obtains the ball, they will be allowed to score.

BOARD AND SPRINT

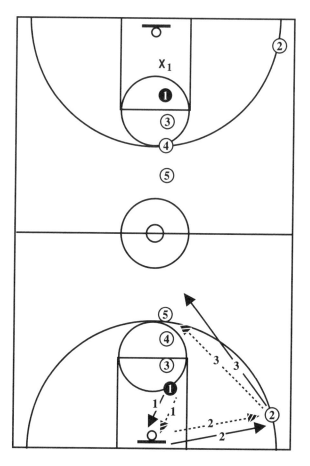

Primary Skill: Rebounding

Objective: To develop rebound and outlet skills.

Equipment Needed: One basketball.

Coaching Tips to Players: Make sharp crisp passes.

Diagram Notes: Upper court illustrates the drill with a defender for more challenge.

Procedure:

- The team splits in half to establish groups of five or six players.
- One unit goes to each end with a basketball.
- O1 starts play by tossing the ball high against the backboard. O1 now jumps up and attempts to grab the rebound at the height of the leap, comes down, pivots on the foot nearest the O2, fires a red hot pass to O2, then sprints to O2's vacated spot.
- O2 yells "Outlet" as soon as O1 grabs the rebound, receives the ball from O1, passes it on to O3, and runs to the end of the rebounding line.
- O3 continues the routine by following the actions of O1.
- O4 and O5 take one step forward each time a rebounder goes after the ball.
- Switch sides after each player has rebounded a given total of times.

OPTIONAL: The rebounder attempts to pass the ball to the outlet person while still in the air.

OPTIONAL: Add a defensive player and give the offense only five seconds to shoot.

CAPTAIN HOOK

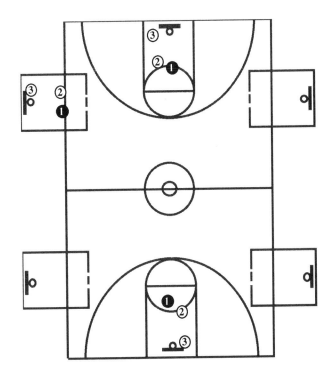

Primary Skill: Rebounding

Objective: To develop the rebound and strong put back.

Equipment Needed: One basketball for each group.

Coaching Tips to Players:
Keep both hands tight on the ball, elbows out, and the ball close to the chin.

Procedure:

- Players form several groups of three and locate at a basket.
- Each unit will need one basketball.
- O1 tosses or shoots the ball against the backboard.
- O2 steps down the lane, jumps up as high as possible, snares the ball, comes down, then powers back up for the score.
- O3 will try to strip the ball from O2.
- Repeat this phase three times.
- Switch sides and repeat the drill.
- Players rotate positions after a predetermined number of put backs.

OPTIONAL: Place two defensive players against O2.

OPTIONAL: Allow the defender to apply tough defense. If the shot is missed, action will continue until either player scores.

CHINA WALL

Primary Skill: Rebounding

Objective: To keep the offensive team from getting a rebound.

Equipment Needed: One basketball for the coach.

Coaching Tips to Players:
Attempt to maintain body contact with the offensive player.

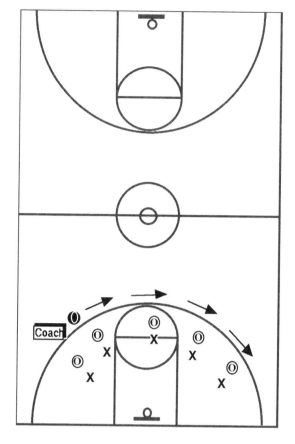

Procedure:

- Players form pairs inside the three-point arc.
- The coach shoots the ball from an assortment of locations.
- The defense blocks out the offense as soon as the ball is shot.
- Play a game to eleven points with the scoring as follows:
  a. One point for the defense getting the rebound.
  b. Two points for the offense getting the rebound.
  c. Two points for the defense allowing the ball to bounce three or more times before getting the rebound.
  d. Three points for the defense allowing the ball to quit bouncing and start rolling.
- After a winner is declared, switch roles and repeat the drill.

OPTIONAL: Give the defense one extra player.

OPTIONAL: Assign a predetermined number of laps or sprints to the losing team.

CIRCLE BLOCK OUT

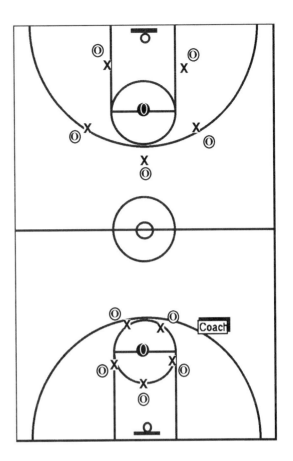

Primary Skill: Rebounding

Objective: To develop team rebounding skills.

Equipment Needed: One basketball placed in the middle of the group.

Coaching Tips to Players: Maintain body contact.

Diagram Notes: Upper court illustrates the optional spread formation.

Procedure:

- The team divides into an offensive and defensive unit.
- Defensive players position themselves around any circle on the floor.
- Match up the defense against the offense.
- Place a stationary ball in the middle of the ring.
- On the whistle or when the word "Shot" is yelled, the defense must hinder the offense from getting to the ball for three seconds.
- Players switch positions after every three skirmishes.

OPTIONAL: Spread the circle out another five feet.

OPTIONAL: Bounce the ball in the middle.

OPTIONAL: Hold the offense out for five seconds.

OPTIONAL: Add one extra defender.

OPTIONAL: Start play with all players sitting.

CLOAKED

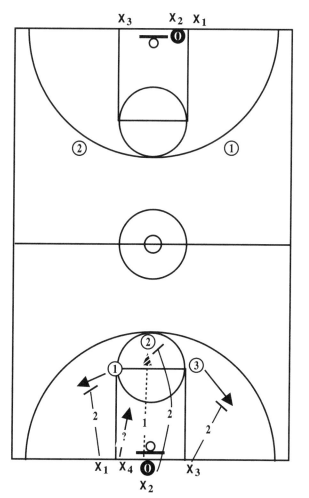

Primary Skill: Rebounding

Objective: To prevent the offense from getting the rebound.

Equipment Needed: One basketball for each group.

Coaching Tips to Players: Communicate and help out whenever possible.

Diagram Notes: Upper court depicts the optional three against two set.

Procedure:

- Three offensive players go against four defensive players.

- The defense blocks out the offense and attempts to let the ball bounce as many times as possible.

- **Excellence** is attained when the ball bounces three or more times.

- **Perfection** is reached when the ball quits bouncing and starts rolling.

- O1, O2, and O3 are on the foul line facing the baseline. One of them receives the ball from a baseline player and immediately shoots it. If the first shot is made, then there is a redo. If the initial shot is missed, O1, O2, and O3 crashes the boards to obtain possession.

OPTIONAL: Go three defenders against two offensive players.

OPTIONAL: Put three against three.

OPTIONAL: Move O1, O2, and O3 out to the three-point line to receive the pass.

CONE DODGE

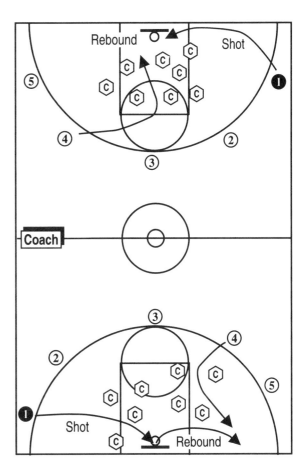

Primary Skill: Rebounding

Objective: To develop body control when rebounding.

Equipment Needed: One ball and eight cones at each end of the court.

Coaching Tips to Players: Move under control.

Procedure:

- Players form two units.
- Each player is assigned a number.
- Units report to opposite ends of the court.
- Position the floor cones all over the floor near the free-throw lane.
- Various players shoot the ball from different areas behind the three-point arc.
- The coach yells out a number. The corresponding player or players immediately go after the rebound by weaving through the cones. The ball should not hit the floor nor should any of the cones be touched by the rebound.
- The rebounder turns and gives the ball to any player on the perimeter.
- Perimeter players shoot from dissimilar areas.

OPTIONAL: Remove the cones from the floor. The player who gets the rebound tries to score a basket.

DASHBOARD

Primary Skill: Rebounding

Objective: To quickly control the ball.

Equipment Needed: One basketball and two cones for each group.

Coaching Tips to Players:
Grab the ball at the highest point of the jump.

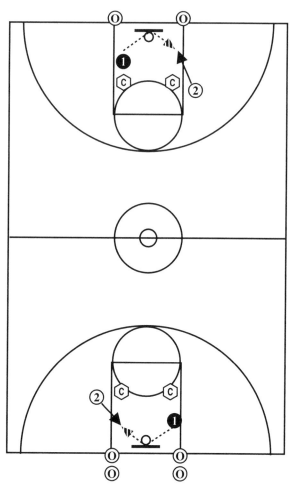

Procedure:

- The team divides into foursomes and each group goes to a basket.

- Two players perform while the other two wait, watch, or rest.

- Establish a location for the floor cones.

- O1 starts by giving two pump fakes, jumping up and shooting the ball against the backboard so that it travels over the rim. After landing, O1 sprints around the cone, returns to jump up and grab the shot or pass from O2, comes down with the ball, gives two pump fakes, and repeats the routine.

- O2 will grab the rebound, come down with it, give two pump fakes, shoot the ball against the backboard over top of the rim to O1, sprint around the cone, return and repeat the process.

- Pairs switch after each player has run around the cone five times.

OPTIONAL: Move the cones to different locations. They do not have to be symmetrical.

FINGER TIPS

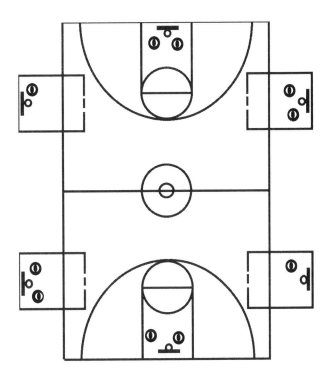

Primary Skill: Rebounding

Objective: To develop ball control during a rebound.

Equipment Needed: One ball for each player.

Coaching Tips to Players:
Keep the hands relaxed.

Procedure:

- Each player gets a basketball and one-half of a backboard.
- Play begins by lobbing the ball against the face of the backboard. They then leap up and at the peak of the jump, tip it against the backboard. They repeat this procedure five times in a row and on the sixth leap, attempt to tap the ball in for a score.
- Methods for tipping include
  a. Right hand only
  b. Left hand only
  c. Alternate hands
  d. Both hands
- Players switch sides and repeat the drill.

OPTIONAL: Players may pair up to allow for a rest period after each tip session.

OPTIONAL: Use a wall instead of the backboard.

KANGAROO

Primary Skill: Rebounding

Objective: To develop rebound timing and the aggressive put back.

Equipment Needed: One ball for each group.

Coaching Tips to Players: After grabbing the ball, make good upper body fakes.

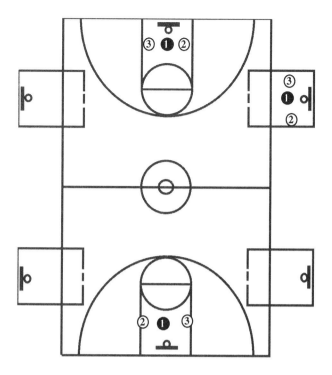

Procedure:

- Players divide into groups of three and go to the basketball key.

- Players should be able to jump about the same height.

- O1 is the referee and timekeeper and also tosses the ball up (jump ball) to start a game, when the ball goes out of bounds, or a basket is made. Play is otherwise continuous.

- Dribbling is prohibited.

- O2 and O3 are rebounders and will stand next to O1. O2 and O3 will jump up, grapple for possession, then without dribbling, attempt to score. The defender attempts to prevent the score. If the shot is missed, play continues.

- The ball is forfeited if held for more than five seconds.

- Three free-throw shots are awarded for any foul.

- Players rotate when either player scores six points. The winner can stay or rest.

OPTIONAL: The winner may elect to stay and play or rest and referee.

LINE TIPS – ONE

Primary Skill: Rebounding

Objective: To develop ball control and rebounding skills.

Equipment Needed: One ball and one floor cone for each group.

Coaching Tips to Players: Handle the rebound at the highest point of the jump.

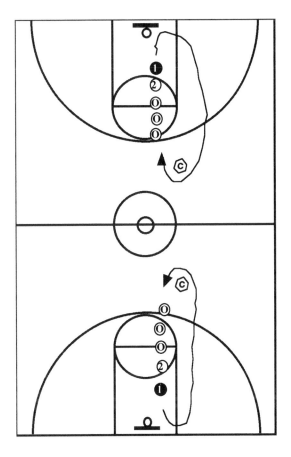

Procedure:

- Players divide into groups and line up in each free-throw lane.

- Each line has a basketball and a floor cone.

- This drill is continuous.

- O1 tosses a ball against the backboard, encircles the cone, and rejoins the line.

- O2 follows O1, jumps up, grabs the ball, comes down with it, goes back up, tips the ball against the backboard, and also sprints around the cone to return to the line.

- All of the other players mimic the first two.

- The ball should never touch the floor.

- After a predetermined number of circuits or time, the ball is tipped in for a basket.

OPTIONAL: Move the cones to different locations.

OPTIONAL: Do not allow the ball to be returned to the floor. Instead, it will be constantly tipped against the glass while each participant is still airborne.

LINE TIPS – TWO

Primary Skill: Rebounding

Objective: To develop ball control and rebounding skills.

Equipment Needed: One ball for each line and two floor cones.

Coaching Tips to Players: Handle the rebound at the highest point of the jump.

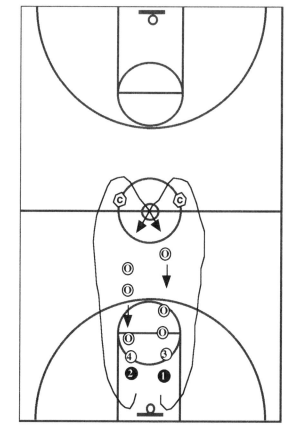

Procedure:

- Players stand in two lines in the key.
- Each line has a basketball and two floor cones.
- This drill is continuous.
- O1 and O2 simultaneously toss their basketballs against the face of the backboard, then sprint around the corresponding cones to the opposite line.
- O3 and O4, jump up, grab the ball, come down with it, go back up, flip the ball off the backboard, then also dash around the cones to the opposing line.
- The ball should never touch the floor.
- After a predetermined number of circuits, the ball is tipped in for a basket.

OPTIONAL: Move the cones to different locations. They do not have to be identical.

OPTIONAL: Do not allow the ball to be brought down. Instead, it is constantly tipped against the glass while each participant is in the air.

ONE MORE TIME

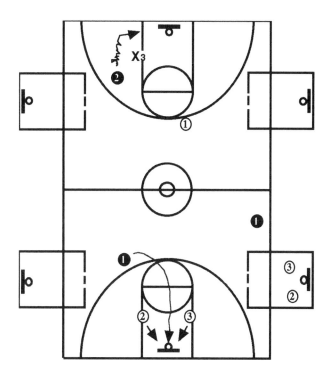

Primary Skill: Rebounding

Objective: To obtain the rebound and score.

Equipment Needed: One basketball for every three players.

Coaching Tips to Players: Be very aggressive.

Procedure:

- Players get into groups of three with one basketball.

- O1 attempts a three-point shot. If made, three points are awarded and O1 shoots again. On a miss, the other two players go for the rebound and O1 remains.

- The player who snares the missed shot has 10 seconds to score against the other.

- If the player who snares the rebound runs out of time, one pass is allowed back to O1 for an additional 10 seconds. When O1 passes the ball back, O1 joins in on defense for a two-against-one. The defender may not steal the ball that was passed back from O1.

- Any score allows that player to go to or remain at the three-point line to start the next series.

- The winner is the first player to score a predetermined amount of points.

OPTIONAL: Do not allow dribbling during the contest.

OUTLETS

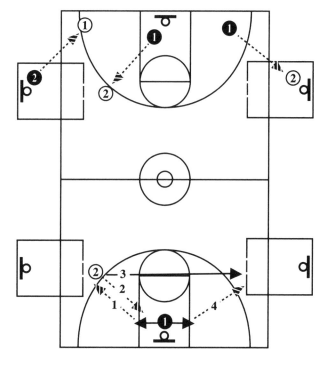

Primary Skill: Rebounding

Objective: To develop rebounding and outlet skills.

Equipment Needed: One ball for every two players.

Coaching Tips to Players: Go up strong and grab the ball with both hands.

Procedure:

- Players pair up with a teammate, then select one ball and go to a basket.
- This is an ongoing drill.
- O1 flips the ball off the backboard, retrieves it from the other side, and outlet passes the ball to O2.
- O2 receives the pass from O1, immediately passes it back to O1, then sprints to the opposite side for the return outlet pass.
- O1 receives the return pass from O2, hurls the ball off the backboard to the other side, rebounds it, then outlet passes it back to O2.
- Players switch positions after several outlets or a predetermined amount of time.

OPTIONAL: After a given number of passes, allow O2 to shoot the ball.

OPTIONAL: After a predicted tally of passes, allow O1 to launch the ball. O2 will grab the rebound, made or missed, and begin the outlet passes.

© 1999 by Parker Publishing Company

OUTLETS AND REBOUNDS

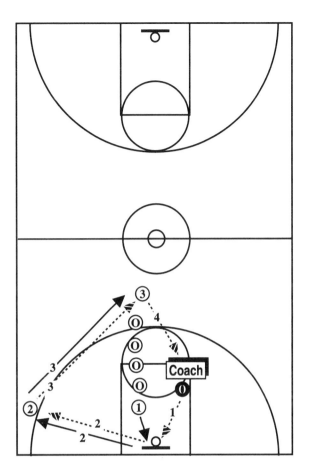

Primary Skill: Rebounding

Objective: To develop the outlet for the fast break.

Equipment Needed: One or two basketballs.

Coaching Tips to Players: After grabbing the rebound, pivot on the outside foot, then outlet the pass.

Procedure:

- Line up the team on one end of the court.

- This is a never ending drill.

- To start play, the coach lofts the basketball off the backboard.

- O1 jumps up high into the air, rebounds the ball at the highest point of the jump, lands, pivots on the foot nearest the outlet person, throws the outlet pass to O2, then sprints to the recently vacated site of O2.

- O2 receives the pass from O1, quickly passes the ball to O3, then runs to the spot where O3 just was standing.

- O3 receives the pass from O2, passes the ball on to the coach, moves up one position in line, and the drill is repeated.

- Each person in line moves up one position after the rebounder leaves.

OPTIONAL: Attempt to turn in the air and outlet the ball before landing on the floor.

OUTLETS – ONGOING

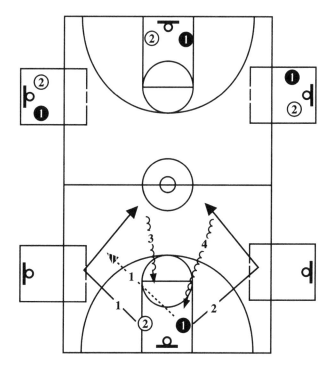

Primary Skill: Rebounding

Objective: To develop the outlet for the fast break.

Equipment Needed: One basketball for each group.

Coaching Tips to Players: Keep the ball, arms, and elbows up.

Procedure:

- Players pair up with a teammate, get a basketball and go to a backboard.

- This is a continuous movement drill.

- O1 tosses the ball against the backboard, rebounds it, pivots on the foot nearest to the partner, then outlet passes the ball to O2.

- As soon as O1 flips the ball off the backboard, O2 takes off on a 45-degree angle toward the sideline, cuts toward the middle at another 45-degree angle, yells "Outlet," receives the pass from O1, stops, dribbles back to the basket, flips the ball off the backboard, rebounds it, and outlet passes to O1.

- O1 will now mimic the above routine of O2.

- Players repeat this process a set number of times.

OPTIONAL: Allow shooting. The ball will be quickly taken out of bounds on any made shots. All missed shots are rebounded by the shooter and immediately passed to the outlet.

© 1999 by Parker Publishing Company

POGO STICK

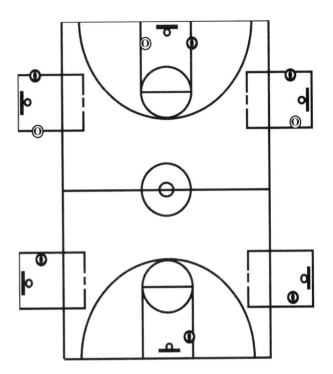

Primary Skill: Rebounding

Objective: To develop rebound timing.

Equipment Needed: One ball for each group.

Coaching Tips to Players:
After grabbing the ball, do not bring the arms and hands down.

Diagram Notes: Upper three courts illustrate the partner option for added challenge.

Procedure:

- Each player gets a basketball and uses one side of a backboard. (Two players may practice this drill on opposite sides of any backboard.)
- Each player begins by tossing the ball high off the backboard.
- Next steps are to jump up, grab the ball, come down, immediately spring back up, then shoot the ball off the glass.
- Players repeat this routine a predetermined number of times.
- Scoring is not allowed.

NOTE: It is very important to use the ankles during the jump and put-back.

OPTIONAL: Allow scoring after a predetermined number of rebounds.

OPTIONAL: Pair up and have one player pass the ball across the backboard above the rim. The other player will jump up, grab the ball, come down, spring back up, and pass the ball back. Each player should repeat this a predetermined number of times without a mistake.

READING THE REBOUND

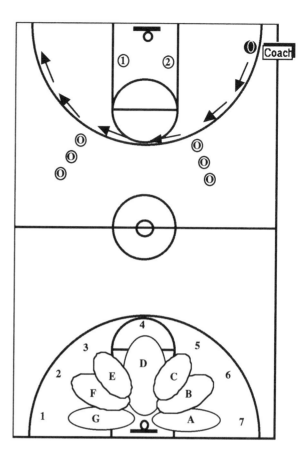

Primary Skill: Rebounding

Objective: To develop player awareness as to where a rebound is most likely to go.

Equipment Needed: One basketball for the coach.

Coaching Tips to Players: Play the percentages by going to one of the two most likely zones.

Procedure:

- The coach shoots from the numbers. O1 and O2 go to the proper zones for the rebound.

- The zones are based on percentages. Stray rebounds will occur.

- When a shot is taken from _____, the rebound usually goes to zone _____ or _____.

1	A	G
2	F	B
3	E	C
4	D	
5	C	E
6	B	F
7	G	A

OPTIONAL: Two more players are added to create an offense and a defensive unit.

ROTTEN EGG

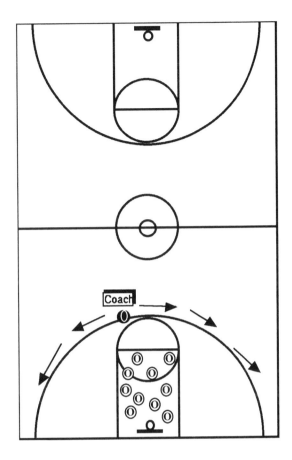

Primary Skill: Rebounding

Objective: To develop aggressiveness for rebounding the ball.

Equipment Needed: One basketball for the coach.

Coaching Tips to Players: Read where the ball will possibly go.

Procedure:

- All players go to one basket.
- The coach shoots the ball.
- On the missed shot, everyone scrambles for the rebound.
- The player who gains control gives the ball back to the coach and goes elsewhere to practice.
- Everyone else goes back to the same basket with the coach repeating the drill.
- Players will try not to be the last person left.

OPTIONAL: The last player remaining will have to do something such as:

a. Run a predetermined number of sprints or laps.

b. Sweep the floor before the next practice.

c. Write a one-paragraph letter of apology for being the last.

SKY HIGH

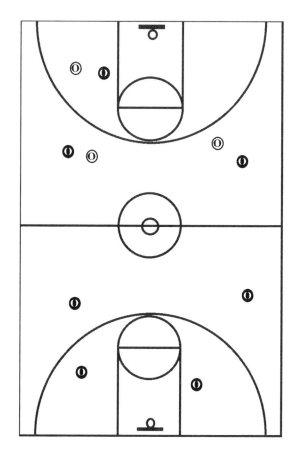

Primary Skill: Rebounding

Objective: To develop rebound timing.

Equipment Needed: One ball for each player.

Coaching Tips to Players: Grab the ball at the highest point of the jump.

Diagram Notes: Upper court illustrates the drill with the use of a partner for greater challenge.

Procedure:

- Every player will need a basketball. Players scatter out all over the floor.
- The ball is tossed 15 to 20 feet into the air.
- Let the ball come down, hit the floor, and bounce back up again.
- The rebounder jumps up and grabs the ball with both hands.
- Players should attempt to grab the ball at the highest point of the jump.
- Practice this routine 10 times.

OPTIONAL: Upon grabbing the ball, shoot it back into the air before coming down. Play is thus continuous. Repeat this exercise five times.

OPTIONAL: Pair up and have the partner underhand pass it into the air. Jump up and grab the ball as before.

OPTIONAL: Pair up and have the partner toss the ball into the air. Jump up, grab the ball and before coming back down, pass the ball back to the partner.

T-REX

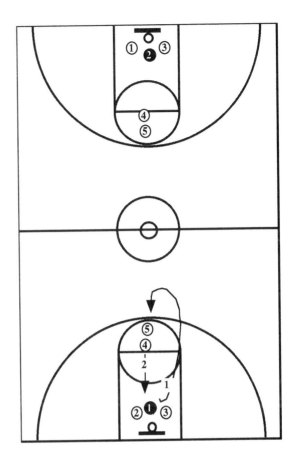

Primary Skill: Rebounding

Objective: To grab the rebound and put the shot back up.

Equipment Needed: One basketball for each group.

Coaching Tips to Players: Use good body fakes.

Procedure:

- The team splits into two groups.
- Each group selects a different basket.
- Play never stops. Even on a made basket, players attempt to get the ball and score.
- Players may take only one dribble before shooting.
- Fouls will send that player to the line for two shots.
- A player may possess the ball for only five seconds. Violators will relinquish the ball and go to the end of the line.
- O1, O2, and O3 fight for the rebound, made or missed, until one of them gets it. An example would be that O1 gets the rebound and scores against O2 and O3. O4 immediately joins O2 and O3 to control the rebound. O1 then travels to the foul line and waits behind O5.
- The first player to reach a predetermined score is the winner.

TEN CHANCES

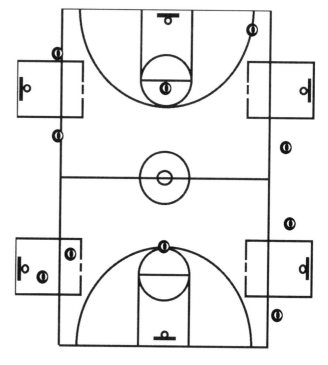

Primary Skill: Rebounding

Objective: To learn to follow the shot for the possible rebound.

Equipment Needed: One ball for each player.

Coaching Tips to Players: Concentrate on making the shot first, then getting the rebound second.

Procedure:

- Every player gets a basketball.
- No more than three players should be at any one basket if at all possible.
- Each player shoots 10 shots.
- Players immediately rebound the errant shot for a quick put-back.
- Players shoot a variety of shots such as
    a. Jump
    b. Hook
    c. Double clutch
    d. Reverse lay-ins
    e. Fade away
    f. Backboard only

OPTIONAL: Players must shoot the first shot with their weak hand.

© 1999 by Parker Publishing Company

Section 11

SHOOTING

You may be disappointed if you fail,
but you are doomed if you don't try.

—Beverly Sills

BANK ON IT

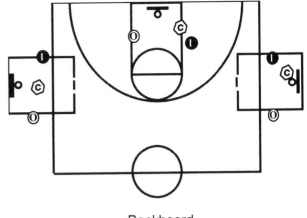

Primary Skill: Shooting

Objective: To develop the skill of using the backboard when shooting an angled shot.

Equipment Needed: One ball and one cone for each group.

Coaching Tips to Players: Focus on the backboard targets.

Backboard

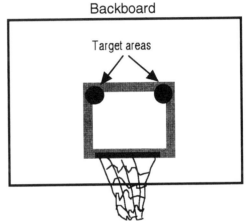

Target areas

Procedure:

- Each player pairs up with someone of choice.
- After grabbing a basketball and a floor cone, each pair goes to a basket.
- One player is the shooter and the other is the rebounder.
- Players take turns shooting five shots in a row from 5 feet away.
- With each return to the shooting position, players move back three feet.
- Each attempts to:
  a. Make four out of five each time.
  b. Make a predetermined number in a row without a miss. Only five at a time may be shot.
  c. Make more than the teammate.
- Partners switch sides and repeat the drill.

BANKER'S HOURS

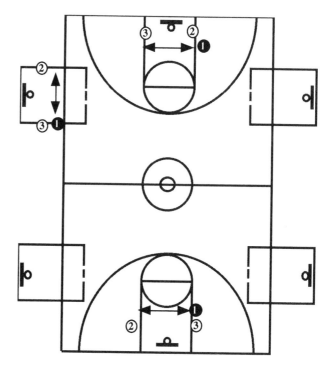

Primary Skill: Shooting

Objective: To improve the ability to make a basket by using the backboard.

Equipment Needed: Two balls for each group of three.

Coaching Tips to Players: Focus on the target spot.

Procedure:

- Players form groups of three.
- Two basketballs are needed for each group.
- The object is to make as many baskets in a row as possible.
- O1 shoots backboard shots from about 10 feet away. First O1 shoots a bank shot from the right side, then rapidly moves across to the left side, picks up the ball from the floor, shoots a bank shot, rapidly moves across to the right side, and repeats the skill.
- O2 and O3 are the rebounders. They quickly return each ball to an exclusive spot on the floor.
- After a predetermined amount of time, or a specific number of made baskets, the three rotate positions.

OPTIONAL: Each player tries to make as many as possible in one minute.

OPTIONAL: The two basketballs may be placed at different locations on the floor.

© 1999 by Parker Publishing Company

CLASH OF THE TITANS

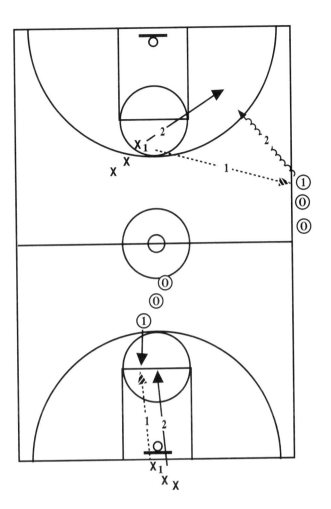

Primary Skill: Shooting

Objective: To develop the ability to get open for a shot.

Equipment Needed: One ball per group.

Coaching Tips to Players:
Make exaggerated fakes.

Diagram Notes: Each court shows optional ways of positioning.

Procedure:

- The defender rolls the ball to O1 and attempts to prevent O1 from scoring.

- O1 picks up the ball and has 10 seconds in which to score. If O1 rebounds the missed shot, 10 more seconds will be awarded.

- O1 can use these steps:
    a. Jab or rocker—fake forward with one foot and the ball, pull back, and shoot.
    b. Jump stop and crossover—stop with both feet simultaneously, then step across the body with the outside foot toward the basket.
    c. Reverse spin—while dribbling, reverse the direction of travel by spinning backwards and pulling the ball across the body.
    d. Reverse pivot—jump stop and spin backwards on the foot closest to the rim.
    e. Combinations—combine a series of steps and moves.

- Switch lines once the drill has been completed.

CONCENTRATION

Primary Skill: Shooting

Objective: To enhance the ability to focus on making the shot.

Equipment Needed: One basketball for each team.

Coaching Tips to Players: Hustle for the rebound.

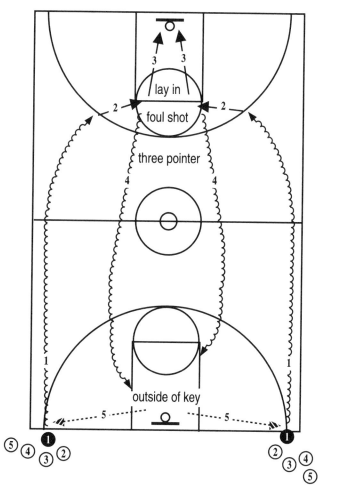

Procedure:

- Players divide into two teams.
- Each team gets one basketball.
- The object is to be the first team to get everyone through the circuit.
- The first player on each team dribbles to the other end, shoots a three pointer, then a foul shot, and finally a lay-in. Only three attempts are permitted to make each shot.
- Next, the player dribbles back for a shot from anywhere **outside** the key. This shot must be made before passing the ball to the next person in line.
- Teams switch sides after a winner has been declared.

NOTE: For safety reasons, players going to the far end must dribble near the sides of the court. When returning, they will dribble down the center.

OPTIONAL: Make four teams. Start them at the side near center court. The four teams must go to the same basket first.

CROSSOVERS

Primary Skill: Shooting

Objective: To free up an offensive player.

Equipment Needed: One ball per player.

Coaching Tips to Players: Make a great fake with the ball.

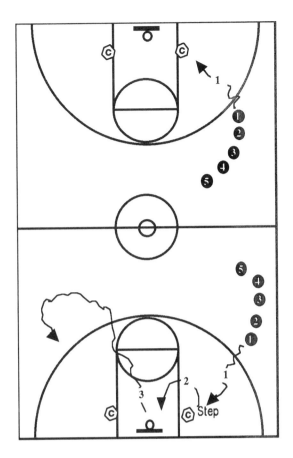

Procedure:

- Each player dribbles to the cone, jump stops, and performs a cross-over step.

ILLUSTRATION OF THE CROSS-OVER

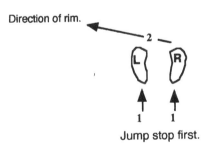

- The foot closest to the basket is the pivot foot. After a great body fake is exhibited, the outside foot steps in front of and across the body toward the basket. The shot is then attempted.
- Alternate from the right and left sides.

DOUBLE DOWN

Primary Skill: Shooting

Objective: To develop skill in delivering an assist for the score.

Equipment Needed: Two basketballs are kept at one end.

Coaching Tips to Players: Concentrate and communicate when working together.

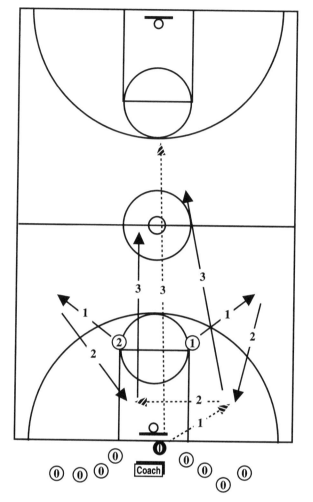

Procedure:

- Players line up in two lines under the basket.
- The coach throws or rolls the ball in any direction.
- O1 and O2 face the coach and stutter-step out and back.
- As soon as the ball is rolled, one player yells "ball" and goes after it.
- The participant who retrieves the ball, passes it to the partner for a lay-in.
- The coach then grabs the ball and tosses it down court. O1 and O2 sprint after it, and work together to make a lay-in at the other end.
- The next two players in line go to the foul line and replicate the actions of the previous two.

NOTE: For safety reasons, make sure that all players return along the sidelines.

OPTIONAL: During the first phase, O1 and O2 are against each other. Either person has only five seconds to score.

FORM SHOOTING – BASKET

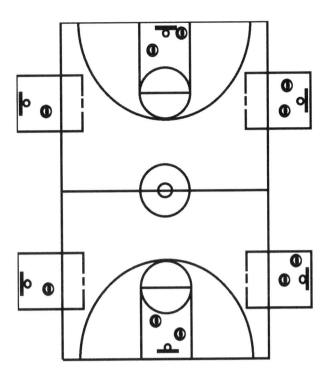

Primary Skill: Shooting

Objective: To develop proper shooting form.

Equipment Needed: One basketball for each player.

Coaching Tips to Players: Concentrate on all of the elements.

Procedure:

- All players stand about five feet away from a basketball rim with a ball.
- The ball will be supported in one hand using the proper shooting form. The other hand is at the shooter's side.
- Each player attempts to make a predetermined number of baskets.
- Each then switches hands and repeats the drill.
- Players will attempt to make a basket while concentrating on "BEEF":
  a. The "B" depicts maintaining proper **balance** with the body.
  b. The first "E" stands for fixing the **eye** on the rim or target. The backboard is the target when shooting from the side.
  c. The second "E" represents keeping the **elbow** under the ball.
  d. The "F" denotes the **follow** through with the wrist.

OPTIONAL: After every five attempts, players will move back two feet and repeat the drill.

FORM SHOOTING – FLOOR

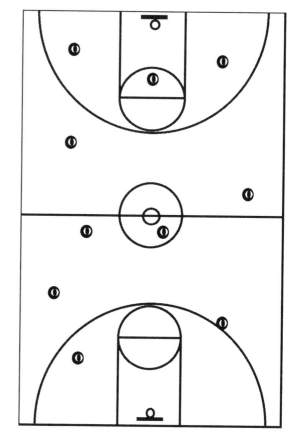

Primary Skill: Shooting

Objective: To develop proper shooting form.

Equipment Needed: One basketball for each player.

Coaching Tips to Players:
Concentrate on all of the elements.

Procedure:

- Each player will need a basketball.
- All players are to lie with their back on the floor.
- Using the proper shooting technique, they will shoot the ball five to ten feet above the head.
- The goal is to catch the returning basketball without moving the hands.
- They will perform this stunt for two minutes.
- Players will shoot the basketball into the air while concentrating on the term "**BEEF**":
    a. The "**B**" depicts maintaining proper **balance** with the body.
    b. The first "**E**" stands for fixing the **eye** on the rim or target. The backboard would be the target when shooting from the side.
    c. The second "**E**" represents keeping the **elbow** under the ball.
    d. The "**F**" denotes the **follow** through with the wrist.

OPTIONAL: Shooters may have a standing partner hold out a hand for a target.

FORM SHOOTING – WALL

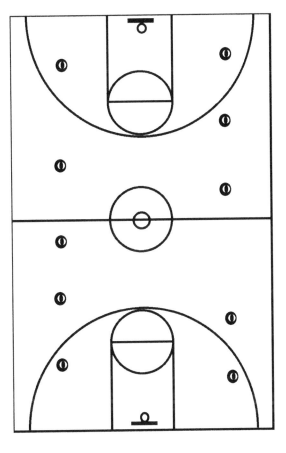

Primary Skill: Shooting

Objective: To develop proper shooting technique.

Equipment Needed: One basketball for each player.

Coaching Tips to Players:
Concentrate on all of the elements.

© 1999 by Parker Publishing Company

Procedure:

- Each player needs a basketball.
- They disperse around the court along a wall and position themselves ten feet from the wall.
- They practice form shooting for two minutes.
- Players shoot at the wall while concentrating on the term "**BEEF**":
  a. The "B" depicts maintaining proper **balance** with the body.
  b. The first "E" stands for fixing the **eye** on the rim or target. The backboard would be the target when shooting from the side.
  c. The second "E" represents keeping the **elbow** under the ball.
  d. The "F" denotes the **follow** through with the wrist.

OPTIONAL: Players may practice using either side of a backboard, especially if wall space is hard to find.

INSIDE OUTSIDE

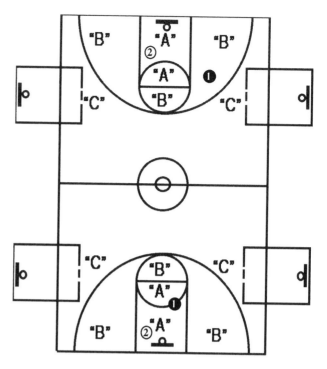

Primary Skill: Shooting

Objective: To develop shooting confidence as fatigue increases.

Equipment Needed: One ball at each basket.

Coaching Tips to Players: Work hard and stay focused.

© 1999 by Parker Publishing Company

Procedure:

- Players pair up at a basket with one basketball between them.
- O1 can shoot the ball only in zone "**A**," on the first go around.
- O2 rebounds and quickly flips the ball anywhere into the "**A**" zone.
- O1 sprints to the ball, grabs it, squares up to the basket, and shoots again.
- This process is repeated 10 times.
- The participants switch roles and duplicate the previous routine.
- After finishing in the "**A**" zone, O1 and O2 should begin the same task in zone "**B**".
- Upon closure in zone "**B**," O1 and O2 should commence the exact assignment in zone "**C**".

OPTIONAL: Require a specific type of shot be taken. These could include jump shots, hook shots, jump hooks, fade away, double clutch, or backboard only.

JAMMING

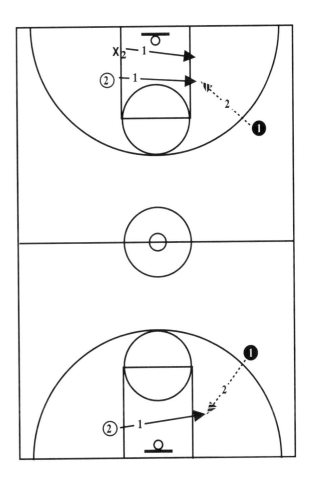

Primary Skill: Shooting

Objective: To develop inside shooting with pressure.

Equipment Needed: One basketball for each group.

Coaching Tips to Players: Give good fakes.

Diagram Notes: Upper court illustrates the drill with a defender for more challenge.

Procedure:

- Players pair up at a basket with one basketball between them.
- O1 passes the ball to O2 as O2 comes across the key and sets up.
- O2 receives the pass, makes a move, then strives to score.
- After a given number of attempts, the players should switch roles.

- Post Moves:
  - a. Jab or rocker step
  - b. Drop step and hook
  - c. Square up and shoot
  - d. Square up and cross over

  Wing moves:
  - a. Jab or rocker step.
  - b. Jump stop with a crossover
  - c. Reverse spin
  - d. Reverse pivot

OPTIONAL: A defensive player can be added against O2. When first learning the moves, X2 should put light pressure against O2 so that maximum confidence and skill development can be attained.

JUMP STOP LAY-INS

Primary Skill: Shooting

Objective: To create teamwork
for the fast break lay-in.

Equipment Needed: One or
two balls at a basket.

Coaching Tips to Players:
Use the glass when attempting the
shot.

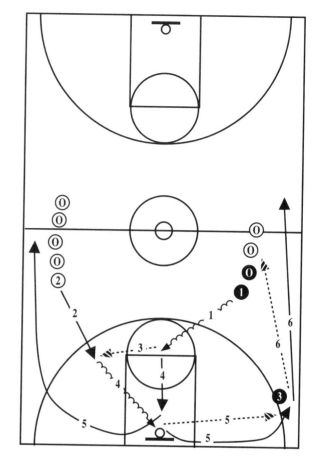

Procedure:

- At middle court, players form two lines, one on each side.

- The coach gives two or three basketballs to one of the lines.

- O1 dribbles to the foul line and jump stops. Next, O1 passes the ball to O2, follows O2 for the rebound, then outlet passes the ball to O3. O1 will now go to the end of the shooting line.

- O2 receives the ball from O1, makes the lay-in, sprints to the side of the court, and takes the place of O3.

- O3 receives the outlet pass from O1, passes the ball to the next person in the dribbling line, and proceeds to the end of this line.

- Flop sides after a given amount of time.

NOTE: This can be used as a warm-up drill.

OPTIONAL: Require that all shots must be off the backboard.

MIKAN

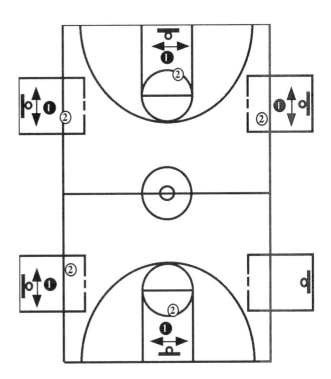

Primary Skill: Shooting

Objective: To develop the hook shot.

Equipment Needed: One ball for every two players.

Coaching Tips to Players:
Keep the elbows and hands up high when rebounding each shot.

Procedure:

- Each player chooses a partner.
- Each pair grabs a ball and goes to a basket.
- O1 stands four to five feet away from the basket and shoots a hook shot.
- O1 immediately gets the rebound and shoots the same shot from the other side.
- Players must keep the hands above the shoulders at all times.
- The ball cannot touch the floor.
- The object is to make a predetermined number of baskets in a row.
- O1 rotates with O2 after 15 to 20 shot attempts.

OPTIONAL: Make as many baskets as possible in a given amount of time.

OPTIONAL: Make more than the partner for a predetermined number of sprints.

OPTIONAL: Shoot lay-ins.

OPTIONAL: Shoot jump hooks.

NOTHING BUT NET

Primary Skill: Shooting

Objective: To improve the
ability to shoot a ball accurately.

Equipment Needed: One
ball and one cone for each
group.

Coaching Tips to Players:
Arch the ball on the shot.

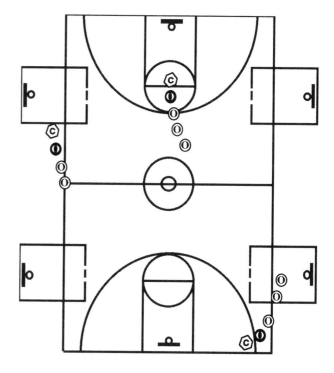

Procedure:

- Players form groups of two or three and use as many baskets as possible.
- Place a floor cone on the court.
- Create a line of players behind the cone.
- Each player shoots one shot, retrieves the rebound, passes the ball to the next person in line, and returns to the end.
- The object is to be the first player to score 11 or more points.
- A nothing-but-net shot is worth three points. All other baskets are worth one point.
- Move the cone to a new location after a completed contest.

OPTIONAL: Form teams and reach a predetermined number of points first.

OPTIONAL: Give each line two basketballs.

OPTIONAL: In order to win, a player must reach exactly 11 points.

OPPONENT'S CHALLENGE

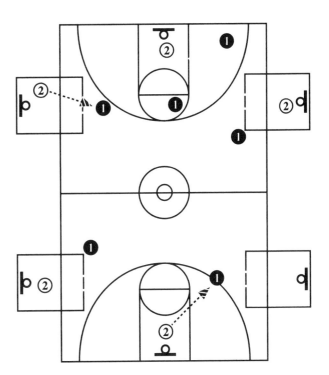

Primary Skill: Shooting

Objective: To develop pressure shooting.

Equipment Needed: One basketball for each group.

Coaching Tips to Players: Concentrate on shooting form.

Procedure:

- Players pair up and select a basket.
- O1 moves about freely and shoots the basketball. When the shot goes in, O1 receives one point. When the shot is missed, the opponent of the next game will receive two points.
- The objective is to reach a predetermined number of points before the opponent.
- An example might be that O1 needs 10 points before the Kennedy High Cougars attain 14 points.
- O2 rebounds each shot and quickly passes the ball back to O1.
- When O1 has finished, players alternate positions and start a new game.

OPTIONAL: Change the point structure to one point for us, and three points for them.

OPTIONAL: Free throws are on a one-and-one basis. If the first shot is made, then the second successful shot is worth two points.

POST MOVES

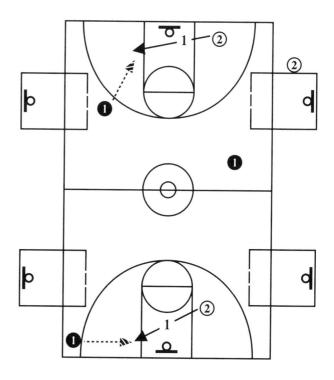

Primary Skill: Shooting

Objective: To free up the post player for a better shot.

Equipment Needed: One ball for each group.

Coaching Tips to Players: Execute great fakes.

Procedure:

- Players pair up and assemble at the various baskets with one ball.

- O2 breaks to a desired spot near the key.

- O1 passes the ball to O2.

- While **facing away from the basket**, O2 receives the ball and executes each of the following moves:

a. Jam	b. Drop and hook	c. Square up	d. Square up and cross over

- Players switch after executing each move five times.

- Players perform the moves from both sides of the key.

OPTIONAL: A defensive player can be added to put pressure on the post player.

268

POSTMASTER

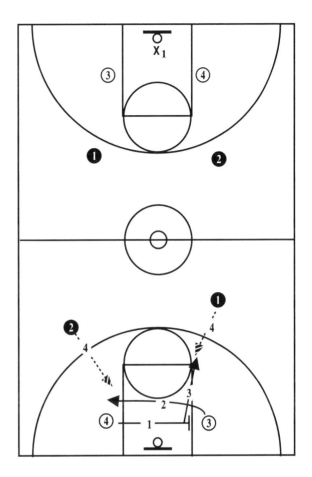

Primary Skill: Shooting

Objective: To develop skills for the open shot.

Equipment Needed: Two basketballs.

Coaching Tips to Players: Give a target with the hand.

Diagram Notes: Upper court illustrates the drill with a defender for more challenge.

Procedure:

- Players form groups of four.
- Each group receives two basketballs.
- Units go to opposite ends of the court.
- O4 screens for O3. After O3 passes, O4 breaks up the key, receives the ball from O1, turns, and shoots one shot.
- O3 moves off the screen set by O4, receives the low pass from O2, turns, and shoots.
- O1 and O2 pass or lob the ball into the post players.
- Post players should take up two new locations along the key each time.
- Players rotate position every ten shots.

OPTIONAL: One defensive player can be added. X1 starts under the basket and chooses either O3 or O4 to play defense against.

OPTIONAL: Two defensive players can be added.

REVERSE PIVOTS

Primary Skill: Shooting

Objective: To free the offensive player for a shot.

Equipment Needed: One basketball for each player and one cone at each basket.

Coaching Tips to Players: Take a quick, but long, step.

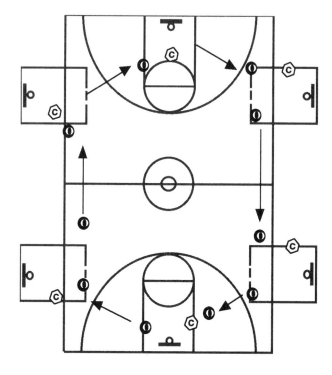

Procedure:

- Everyone dribbles in a clockwise rotation.

- As players approach a cone, they execute a reverse-pivot step, make a lay-in, and proceed to the next basket.

- After a given time, move the cones to the other side of the key and repeat the drill.

SHOOT 'EM UP

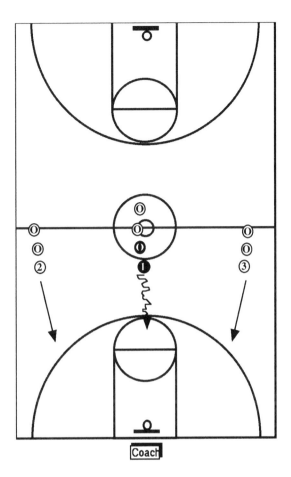

Primary Skill: Shooting

Objective: To develop shooting aggressiveness and tenacity.

Equipment Needed: Two basketballs.

Coaching Tips to Players: Never give up.

Procedure:

- Players form three lines at center court.

- The basketball will be in the center line.

- O1 dribbles down the middle and watches the coach.

- When the coach signals stop, O1 shoots the ball. When the shot is good, either O2 or O3 grabs the ball and the threesome returns to center court via the outside. When the shot is missed, O2 and O3 fight for the rebound and try to score.

- Players have ten seconds to make a shot.

- When the coach signals right or left, O1 passes the ball in that direction.

- The receiver of the pass from O1 shoots the ball.

- O1 and the other player attack the basket and fight for any miscalculated shot.

- Players switch lines after each skirmish.

OPTIONAL: Allow the shooter to reenter the contest on missed shots.

SHOOTING CIRCUIT

Primary Skill: Shooting

Objective: To develop shooting skill and confidence.

Equipment Needed: One basketball for each participant.

Coaching Tips to Players: Use the backboard whenever possible.

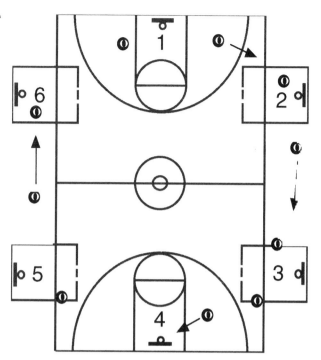

Procedure:

- Players circle the court and perform the following shots at each basket as they dribble by.

    a. Basket #1—Lay-in from over the head using the backboard.

    b. Basket #2—Hook shoot over the front of the rim.

    c. Basket #3—Reverse side lay-up.

    d. Basket #4—Lay in scoop shot off of the glass.

    e. Basket #5—Speed lay-in down the middle.

    f. Basket #6—Jump stop, cross-over step, lay-in from the side.

- Players switch directions after a given amount of time.

- Only one attempt is allowed at each basket. Participants grab their own rebound and dribble on. This is not a race.

OPTIONAL: Change the type of shot at a basket; ten-foot bank, fade away, double clutch, etc.

OPTIONAL: Call out the type of shot to be attempted, forcing quick decisions.

STAR BURST

Primary Skill: Shooting

Objective: To develop shooting under pressure.

Equipment Needed: One ball for each player.

Coaching Tips to Players: Use the backboard when possible.

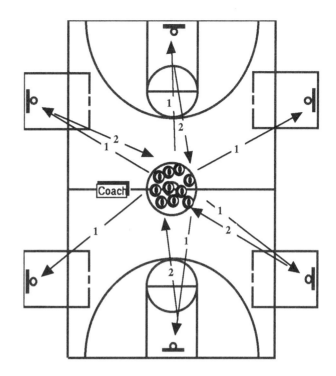

Procedure:

- Each player gets a basketball and enters the center circle.
- Once inside the circle boundary, the entire team begins slowly walking in a clockwise direction.
- When the coach blows the whistle, everybody sprints to a basket of choice.
- Players must make a shot at a hoop before they are allowed to return to the center circle.
- The object is to avoid being one of the last three players back.
- Repeat the drill several times.

OPTIONAL: Allow only backboard shots.

OPTIONAL: Designate areas where the shot must be made.

OPTIONAL: Only a predetermined type of shot may be attempted.

OPTIONAL: Pair up the players. They must return to the circle together or not at all.

STAR BURST PLUS ONE

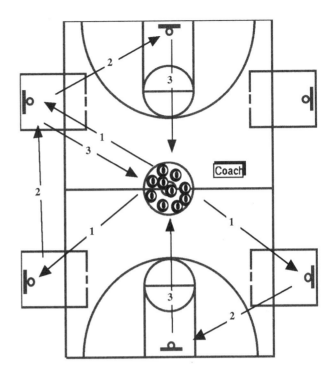

Primary Skill: Shooting

Objective: To develop shooting under pressure.

Equipment Needed: One ball for each player.

Coaching Tips to Players: Stay focused.

Procedure:

- Each player grabs a ball and proceeds to the center circle.

- Once inside the circle boundary, the team begins walking in a clockwise direction.

- When the coach blows the whistle, everybody sprints to any basket and attempts a shot. After the shot is successful, players grab their own rebound and proceed to the next clockwise basket. Once there, they must make a shot before returning to the center circle.

- The object is to avoid being one of the last three players to return to the center circle.

- Repeat the drill several times.

NOTE: To prevent collisions, all players must rotate to the next basket that is located in a clockwise direction.

OPTIONAL: Only a predetermined type of shot may be attempted each time.

OPTIONAL: Pair up the players. They must return to the circle together or not at all.

STOP OR CUT

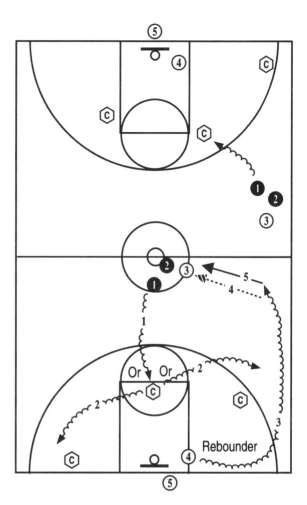

Primary Skill: Shooting

Objective: To develop quick reactions toward unknown situations.

Equipment Needed: Four basketballs and six floor cones.

Coaching Tips to Players: Wait and react accordingly.

Diagram Notes: Upper court illustrates the drill with the ball entering from the side.

Procedure:

- Players break into two groups.
- Cones should be set up at both ends of the court.
- O1 dribbles down the middle.
- O4 hand signals O1 to either stop, go left, or go right.
- O1 executes the order, shoots the shot from behind a cone, and proceeds to under the basket.
- O4 retrieves O1's rebound, dribbles out to the sideline, passes the ball to the next person in line, and goes to the end of the shooting line.
- O2 follows as soon as O1 shoots the ball. O2 will be watching to see what O5's hand signal will be. Play is thus continuous.
- Move the cones periodically to establish new shooting areas.

OPTIONAL: Players will switch ends after rebounding.

THREE-RING CIRCUS

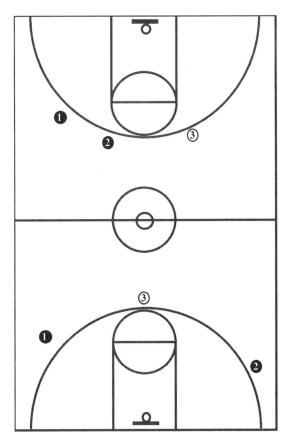

Primary Skill: Shooting

Objective: To develop shooting under pressure and fatigue.

Equipment Needed: Two basketballs per group.

Coaching Tips to Players: Concentrate on the proper shooting form.

Procedure:

- Players form groups of three.

- Each threesome needs two basketballs.

- The coach sets up shooting areas. Examples might be from outside the three-point arc, outside the key, inside the key, or inside the circle.

- The goal is to be the first player to score a predetermined number of baskets.

- Two of the players start the contest by shooting the basketballs at the same time. Both individuals retrieve their rebounds—made or missed—and toss it to the open person. After passing to the open person, they should quickly get to the shooting area to receive the next pass.

- Play is continuous until a winner is declared.

OPTIONAL: Make teams and be the first team to score a predetermined number of baskets.

OPTIONAL: Make teams composed of four players and three basketballs.

TIME OUT

Primary Skill: Shooting

Objective: To develop shooting when fatigued.

Equipment Needed: One ball for every two players.

Coaching Tips to Players:
Use the backboard when possible.

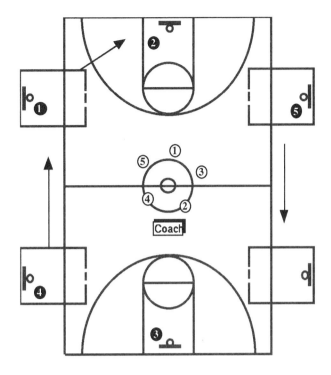

Procedure:

- Players pair up and get one basketball.

- One partner becomes the shooter; the other goes to the center circle.

- Shooters make the identical shot at every basket while rotating in a clockwise direction. Once the circuit is completed, they exchange places with their partner.

- Shots might include backboard, over the rim, foul, hook, jump, outside of the key, use the off hand only, or whatever the coach chooses.

- Players who are in the center do a prescribed task until the partner returns.

- Center tasks might be jumping rope, push-ups, sit-ups, run in place, defensive slides, short sprints, or whatever the coach specifies.

OPTIONAL: Players will switch after a predetermined amount of time.

OPTIONAL: If the court only has two baskets, shooters will have to make four shots before the switch takes place.

UP AND OVER

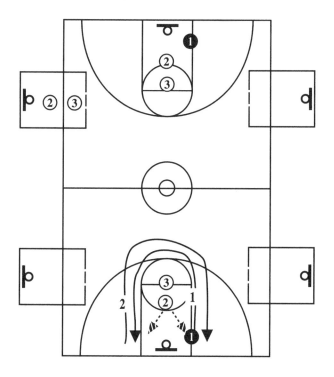

Primary Skill: Shooting

Objective: To develop agility and speed for shooting.

Equipment Needed: One basketball for each group of three or four players.

Coaching Tips to Players: As fatigue sets in, concentrate even harder.

Procedure:

- Players form groups of three.

- Each group needs a basketball and a basket.

- O1 sprints to the ball, grabs it, and attempts a shot. Immediately after the shot, O1 sprints around the stack in the opposite direction created by O2 and O3. O1 again receives the ball from O2 and attempts a shot.

- O2 flips the ball from side to side as O1 nears. O2 is also the rebounder on shots taken by O1.

- O3 is the spacer and can be at any distance desired.

- Players rotate after ten shot attempts.

OPTIONAL: All shots must be against the glass.

OPTIONAL: Only jump shots are allowed.

OPTIONAL: Make the most shots in one minute.

© 1999 by Parker Publishing Company

WHIRLWIND

Primary Skill: Shooting

Objective: To develop shooting confidence when tired.

Equipment Needed: Two basketballs for each group.

Coaching Tips to Players: Concentrate on proper shooting form.

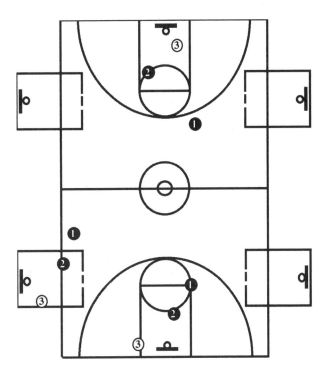

Procedure:

- Players form groups of three.

- Each group gets two basketballs and goes to a basket.

- O1 is the shooter. O1 continuously retrieves the ball, squares up, and shoots the ball from a variety of locations.

- O2 is the passer. As soon as O1 shoots the ball, O2 passes the second ball to a new location so that O1 has to move to retrieve it.

- O3 is the rebounder and passes all rebounds, made or missed, to O2.

- Players rotate positions after a predetermined number of shots have been attempted.

OPTIONAL: Allow each person to shoot the ball for a predetermined amount of time. See which player can make the most baskets from outside a given area. The winner could be within the threesome or the best among the whole team.

Section 12

SIMPLE STATISTICS

*One thing about going the extra mile . . . .
there's never a lot of traffic.*

—Anonymous

SAMPLE TALLY SHEET

Opponent: Kennedy
Location (Home) There
Date: 1-15-98

KEY FOR FLOOR PLAY
10 = 3 point attempt
10 = 3 point made
10 = 2 point attempt
10 = 2 point made
10 D = Defensive rebound
10 O = Offensive rebound
10 + = Got back the ball
10 - = Caused a turnover
10 A = Assisted in a score
10 B = Blocked a shot

KEY FOR FREE THROWS
10 ◯ = Missed   10 ● = Made   10 ⌢ = One and one   10 ◯◯ = Two shots

1st Period 10◯ 15◯●	2nd Period
3rd Period	4th Period

1st Period   10   22R   ㉒   15+   15-   10   22

© 1999 by Parker Publishing Company

Procedure:

1. Fill in the opponent's name, circle the locale, and log in the date.

2. Write down what your players are doing as the events unfold during the game. It will be recorded as if writing the sentences in a paragraph, with the paragraph being each quarter or half.

3. The first line reads like this: 10 shoots and misses, 22 rebounds the ball, 22 shoots and makes a two-point shot, 15 steals the ball from the other team, 15 turns it over to the other team, 10 shoots and makes a three-pointer, and so on.

4. The free throws read like this: 10 shoots one shot and misses, 15 was fouled in the act of shooting and missed the first shot, then made the second.

5. This data will be used to fill in the basketball game statistics sheet. As a number is recorded off this sheet, **draw a line through it** so it will not be used again.

NOTE: It is a good idea to have two statisticians keep this sheet. One watches and writes while the other just watches and helps out.

TALLY SHEET

Opponent: _____
Location   Home - There
Date: _____

KEY FOR FLOOR PLAY

<u>10</u> = 3 point attempt
10 = 3 point made
10 = 2 point attempt
Ⓞ = 2 point made
10 D = Defensive rebound
10 O = Offensive rebound
10 + = Got back the ball
10 - = Caused a turnover
10 A = Assisted in a score
10 B = Blocked a shot

KEY FOR FREE THROWS

10 ◯ = Missed   10 ● = Made   10 ◠ = One and one   10 ◯◯ = Two shots

1st Period	2ndPeriod
3rd Period	4th Period

1st Period
2nd Period
3rd Period
4th Period

SAMPLE SHOT CHART

Opponent: _Kennedy_ (Home) - Away   (1st)- 2nd - 3rd - 4th (Quarter)- Half
Date: _1-15-98_

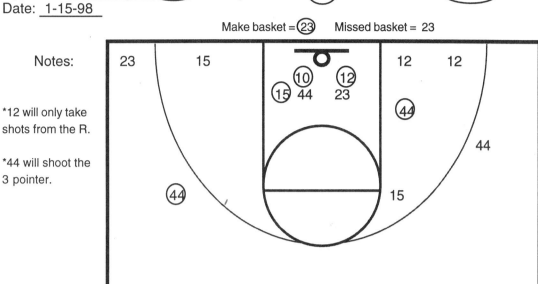

Make basket = (23)   Missed basket = 23

Notes:

*12 will only take
shots from the R.

*44 will shoot the
3 pointer.

Procedure:

1. Make four copies, one for each quarter.

2. Fill in the opponent, circle the location, and fill in the date.

3. Circle the quarter that is being recorded.

4. As the various players shoot the ball, put their uniform number in that spot. If the shot was missed, do not circle the uniform number. If the shot was made, circle the number.

5. At the end of the quarter or the end of the game, put reminders in the notes column beside the floor plan.

SHOT CHART

Opponent: _____ Home - Away 1st - 2nd - 3rd - 4th Quarter - Ha
Date:_____

Make basket = (23) Missed basket = 23

Notes:

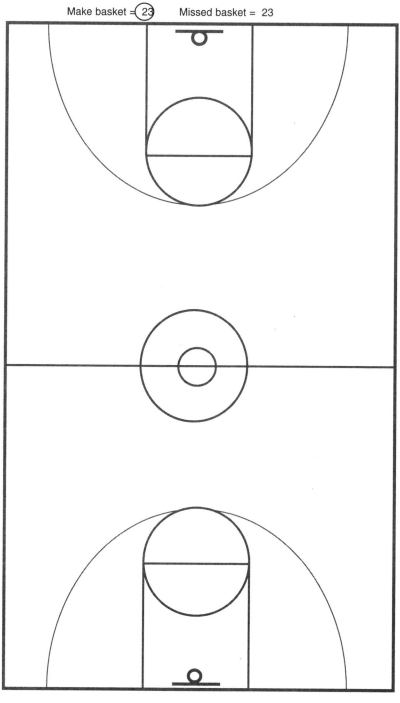

GAME STATISTICS

© 1999 by Parker Publishing Company

Opponent: _____ Home - Away

Date: _____

Note: % = Made divided by try

| Player: | No | Three Point | | | Two Point | | | Free Throw | | | Rebounds | | | Recoveries | Turnovers | Assists | Blocks |
		Try	Made	%	Try	Made	%	Try	Made	%	Off	Def	Total				
Team Totals																	

Note: Divide the made into the try = %

Section 13

SKILL TESTING

No one knows what he can do till he tries

—Publilius Syrus

INSTRUCTIONS FOR TESTING

Equipment Needed:

1. Personal Skill Sheets
2. Data Sheet
3. Stopwatches
4. Masking Tape
5. Basketballs

Skill Test Stations:

1. **Pressure Lay-ins:** Make as many lay-ins as possible in 30 seconds.
2. **Free Throws:** Shoot five (5) at a time and then rotate.
3. **Spot Shooting:** Shoot from the #1 cone and move on when made. Ten tries to make seven different shots.

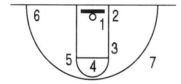

4. **Backboard Bounces:** TIP the ball against the backboard as many times as possible in thirty (30) seconds.
5. **Obstacle Course:** Dribble by as many cones as possible in thirty (30) seconds. The center cone *must be circled* each time it is passed.

6. **Hand Reflexes:** From twelve (12) feet away, toss and catch the ball as many times as possible against the wall in fifteen (15) seconds.
7. **Jump And Reach:** Record the highest jump out of three attempts. Only a one step approach is allowed.
8. **Wall Targets:** From fifteen (15) feet away, hit the target on the wall as many times as possible with fifteen (15) attempts.
9. **Three On Three:** Combine all of the skills of basketball and play in a three (3) to five (5) minute game.

SAMPLE SCORE SHEET

Name ___John Williams___   Height <u>6</u> ft. <u>4</u> in.

List your experiences in basketball prior to this year.

1. <u>Five Star Summer Camp   1997</u>   4. <u>Milrose Middle School   3 years</u>

2. <u>Mike Kovinski Basketball Camp   1996</u>   5. _____

3. <u>Mt. St. Mary High JV   1995</u>   6. _____

Circle the number you make. If you give a false recording, you will be asked to leave immediately. No Exceptions!

Totals

1. Pressure Lay-ins (30 seconds)
   5 6 7 8 9 10 11 12 (13) 14 15 16 17 18 19 20 21 22 23 24 25   13

2. Free throws (20 attempts)
   1 2 3 4 5 6 7 8 9 10 11 12 13 14 (15) 16 17 18 19 20   15

3. Spot Shooting (10 attempts)
   1 2 3 4 5 (6) 7   6

4. Backboard Bounces (30 seconds)
   5 6 7 8 9 10 11 12 13 14 15 16 17 18 19 20 21 22 (23) 24 25   23

5. Obstacle Course (30 seconds)
   5 6 7 8 9 10 11 (12) 13 14 15 16 17 18 19 20 21 22 23 24 25   12

6. Hand Reflexes (15 seconds)
   10 11 12 13 14 15 16 17 18 19 (20) 21 22 23 24 25 26 27 28 29 30   20

7. Jump and Reach (3 attempts)
   7 8 9 10 11 12 13 14 15 16 17 18 19 20 21 22 (23) 24 25 26 27 28   23

8. Wall Targets (15 attempts)
   1 2 3 4 5 6 7 8 9 10 11 (12) 13 14 15   12

9. Three-on-Three (Timed Game)
   1 2 3 (4) 5   4

Shooting Skills Total (add #1 + #2 + #3) =   34

Skill Test Total (add #4 + #5 + #6 + #7 + #*) =   90

292

SCORE SHEET

Name _____   Height __ ft. __ in.

List your experiences in basketball prior to this year.

1. _____   4. _____
2. _____   5. _____
3. _____   6. _____

Circle the number you make. If you give a false recording, you will be asked to leave immediately.
No Exceptions!

Totals

1. Pressure Lay-ins (30 seconds)
   5 6 7 8 9 10 11 12 13 14 15 16 17 18 19 20 21 22 23 24 25 . . . .

2. Free throws (20 attempts)
   1 2 3 4 5 6 7 8 9 10 11 12 13 14 15 16 17 18 19 20 . . . .

3. Spot Shooting (10 attempts)
   1 2 3 4 5 6 7 . . . .

4. Backboard Bounces (30 seconds)
   5 6 7 8 9 10 11 12 13 14 15 16 17 18 19 20 21 22 23 24 25 . . . .

5. Obstacle Course (30 seconds)
   5 6 7 8 9 10 11 12 13 14 15 16 17 18 19 20 21 22 23 24 25 . . . .

6. Hand Reflexes (15 seconds)
   10 11 12 13 14 15 16 17 18 19 20 21 22 23 24 25 26 27 28 29 30 . . . . . .

7. Jump and Reach (3 attempts)
   7 8 9 10 11 12 13 14 15 16 17 18 19 20 21 22 23 24 25 26 27 28 . . . . . .

8. Wall Targets (15 attempts)
   1 2 3 4 5 6 7 8 9 10 11 12 13 14 15 . . . .

9. Three-on-Three (Timed Game)
   1 2 3 4 5 . . . .

Shooting Skills Total (add #1 + #2 + #3) =

Skill Test Total (add #4 + #5 + #6 + #7 + #*) =

© 1999 by Parker Publishing Company

293

SAMPLE SKILLS TEST DATA SHEET #1

Overall Ranking	Name	Pressure Lay-ins	Free Throws	Spot Shooting	Backboard Bounces	Obstacle Course	Hand Reflexes	Jump Reach	Wall Target	Three-on-Three	Shooting Skills Total	Skills Test Total	Grand Total
1	JOHN WILLIAMS	13	15	6	23	12	20	23	12	4	34	90	124
2	BILL THURSTON	8	9	4	14	8	15	18	8	2	21	63	84
3	TIM HALFMUSON	21	19	5	20	19	25	27	11	5	45	102	147

© 1999 by Parker Publishing Company

Instructions:

- This is a very useful and efficient tool for dividing up teams with equal abilities, for making a varsity roster, and for possibly having to cut individuals.
- The **three-on-three** is probably the best overall indicater for the total abilities of any individual during game play.
- Write in the name of each participant.
- Transfer the appropriate scores from their *personal score sheet* to the *comparative data sheet.*
- Compare each individual for their overall ranking.

SKILLS TEST DATA SHEET #1

Overall Ranking	Name	Pressure Lay-ins	Free Throws	Spot Shooting	Backboard Bounces	Obstacle Course	Hand Reflexes	Jump Reach	Wall Target	Three-on-Three	Shooting Skills Total	Skills Test Total	Grand Total
1													
2													
3													
4													
5													
6													
7													
8													
9													
10													
11													
12													
13													
14													
15													
16													
17													
18													
19													
20													
21													
22													
23													
24													
25													
26													
27													
28													
29													
30													

SKILLS TEST DATA SHEET #2

Overall Ranking	Name	Pressure Lay-ins	Free Throws	Spot Shooting	Backboard Bounces	Obstacle Course	Hand Reflexes	Jump Reach	Wall Target	Three-on-Three	Shooting Skills Total	Skills Test Total	Grand Total
31													
32													
33													
34													
35													
36													
37													
38													
39													
40													
41													
42													
43													
44													
45													
46													
47													
48													
49													
50													
51													
52													
53													
54													
55													
56													
57													
58													
59													
60													

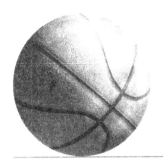

Section **14**

TOURNAMENTS

Opportunities multiply as they are seized.

—Sun Tzu

CREATING A ROUND-ROBIN TOURNAMENT

Procedure:

This arrangement will work with any number of players or teams. Assign a number to each player or team. Put the numbers in the same format as in sample (a). This becomes the first set of games to be played. To create the schedule for game two, just freeze the upper left hand corner number **(1)** and rotate all of the other numbers one position clockwise. This is now the schedule for game two. See sample (b). Continue this methodology and each team will wind up playing every other team once.

(a) 1 vs 2	(b) 1 vs 8	(c) 1 vs 7
8 vs 3	7 vs 2	6 vs 8
7 vs 4	6 vs 3	5 vs 2
6 vs 5	5 vs 4	4 vs 3

If there is an **uneven** number of players or teams, just replace the number 1 with Bye and continue the rotation. Each team will now get a Bye along with having six games. See samples (d), (e), and (f).

(d) **Bye** vs 2	(e) **Bye** vs 8	(f) **Bye** vs 7
8 vs 3	7 vs 2	6 vs 8
7 vs 4	6 vs 3	5 vs 2
6 vs 5	5 vs 4	4 vs 3

This format will work with any number of players or teams as long as the rotation is always in the same direction, either clockwise or counter clockwise. After each game, tally the wins to determine the winner and or placements.

OTHER TOURNAMENT FORMATS

I. *Double Elimination Bracket:*

A player or team must lose **twice** to be eliminated from the tournament.

II. *Single Elimination Bracket:*

A player or team must win to stay in the tournament.

III. *Top Gun:*

1. Winners move up to the next higher location after a projected **time** or **number** of points have been attained.

2. The vanquished will stay at the same spot and take on the next challenger.

3. Once at the **Top Gun** spot, a player or team will attempt to win a predetermined number of games **in a row.** This is usually two or three.

4. Any loss at the top spot will cause that person or team to go to the bottom spot and start over.

5. When a player or team wins the predetermined number at the top locale, s/he must return to the lowest location and start over.

IV. *Total Points:*

1. Record the final score of each game played by a team.

2. Tally all of the scores of each team.

3. Those teams with the highest accumulative totals will be in the Gold Championship bracket. The other teams will vie for the Silver.

© 1999 by Parker Publishing Company

DOUBLE ELIMINATION (8)

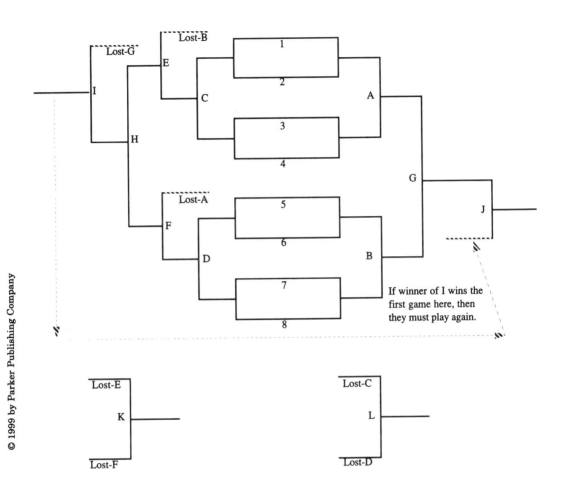

Lost-G

Lost-B

1

2

E

I

C

A

H

3

4

G

5

J

Lost-A

F

6

B

D

7

If winner of I wins the
first game here, then
they must play again.

8

Lost-E

Lost-C

K

L

Lost-F

Lost-D

FINAL STANDINGS

PLACE		NO #	NAME
1st	Won J		
2nd	Lost J		
3rd	Lost I		
4th	Lost H		
5th	Won K		
6th	Lost K		
7th	Won L		
8th	Lost L		

DOUBLE ELIMINATION (16)

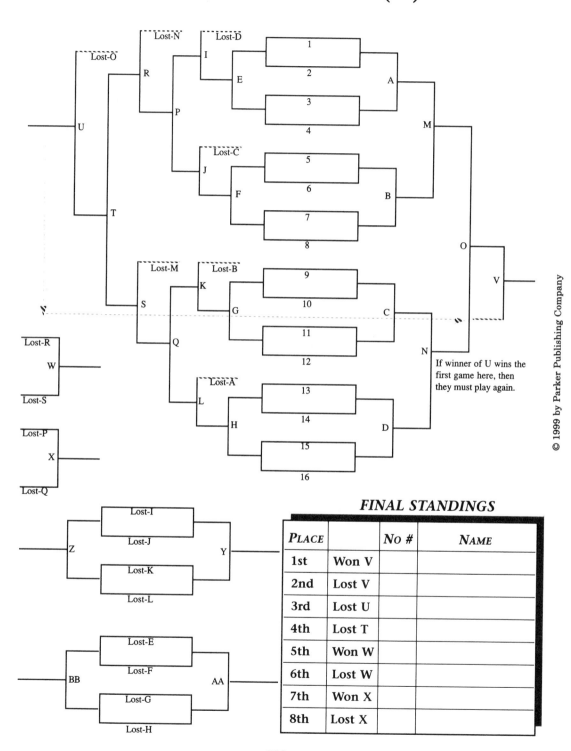

If winner of U wins the first game here, then they must play again.

© 1999 by Parker Publishing Company

FINAL STANDINGS

PLACE		NO #	NAME
1st	Won V		
2nd	Lost V		
3rd	Lost U		
4th	Lost T		
5th	Won W		
6th	Lost W		
7th	Won X		
8th	Lost X		

SINGLE ELIMINATION

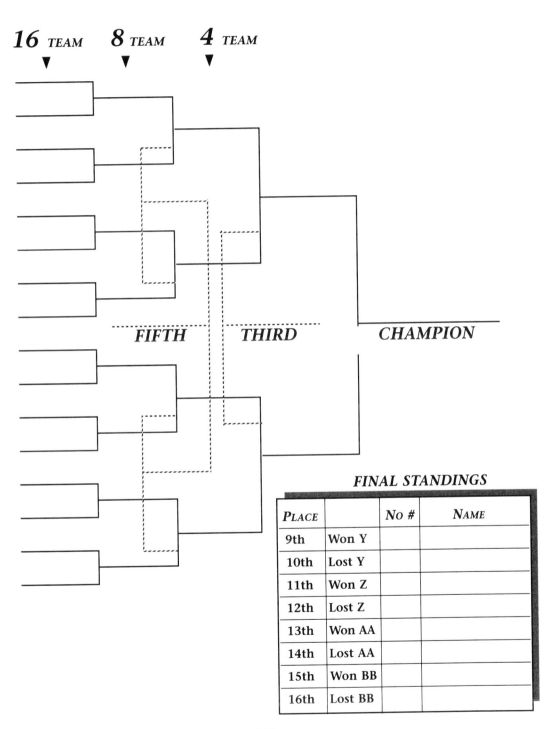

16 TEAM ▼   **8** TEAM ▼   **4** TEAM ▼

FIFTH   *THIRD*   *CHAMPION*

© 1999 by Parker Publishing Company

FINAL STANDINGS

PLACE		No #	NAME
9th	Won Y		
10th	Lost Y		
11th	Won Z		
12th	Lost Z		
13th	Won AA		
14th	Lost AA		
15th	Won BB		
16th	Lost BB		

READY-TO-USE
FORMS

On the day of victory no one is tired.

—Anonymous

PRACTICE SCHEDULE

Date: _____

Floor Plans

Times	Agenda

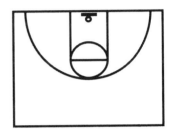

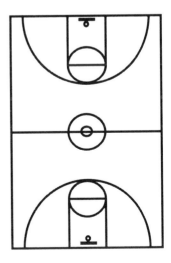

FLOOR PLAN

Information: _____

_____

DEFENSE – PERSON-TO-PERSON

Name: _____

Information: _____
_____
_____
_____
_____
_____

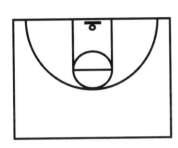  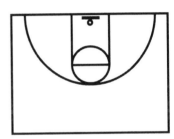

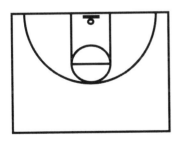  

DEFENSE – ZONE

Name: _____

Information: _____

_____

_____

_____

_____

_____

_____

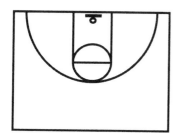  

OFFENSE – PERSON-TO-PERSON

Name: _____

Information: _____
_____
_____
_____
_____
_____

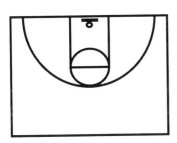

OFFENSE – ZONE

Name: _____

Information: _____
_____
_____
_____
_____
_____
_____

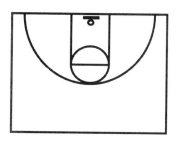
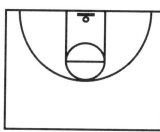
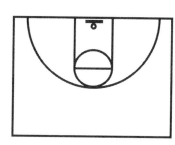

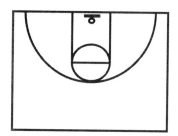
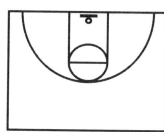

PRESS – DEFENSIVE FULL COURT

Name: _____

Information: _____
_____
_____
_____
_____
_____
_____

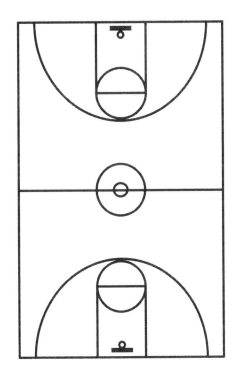

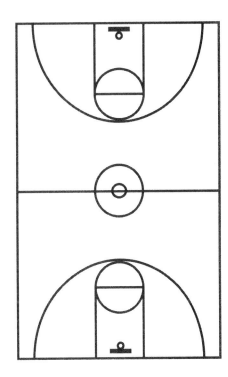

PRESS – DEFENSIVE HALF COURT

Name: _____

Information: _____
_____
_____
_____
_____
_____
_____

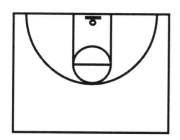

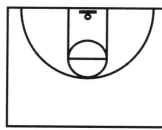

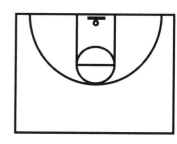

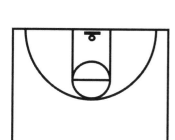

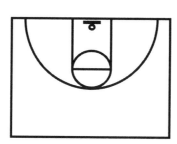

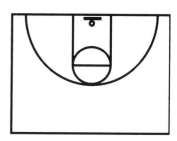

PRESS – OFFENSIVE FULL COURT

Name: _____

Information: _____
_____
_____
_____
_____
_____
_____

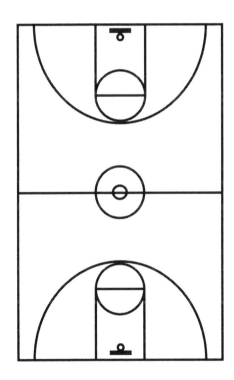
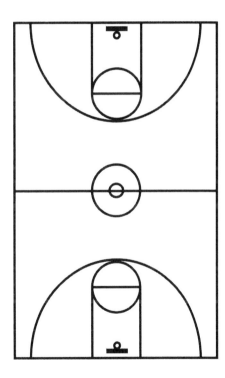

PRESS – OFFENSIVE HALF COURT

Name: _____

Information: _____
_____
_____
_____
_____
_____

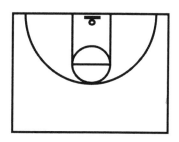
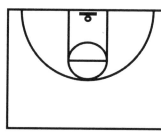
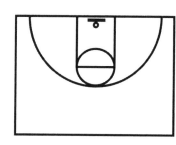

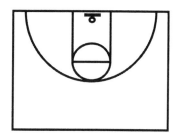
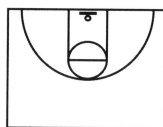
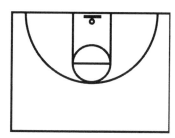

FAST BREAK

Name: _____

Information: _____
_____
_____
_____
_____
_____
_____

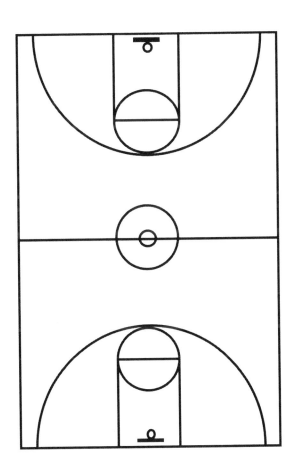

IN BOUNDS

Name: _____

Information: _____
_____
_____
_____
_____
_____
_____

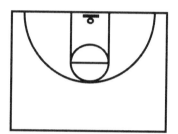
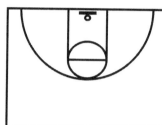

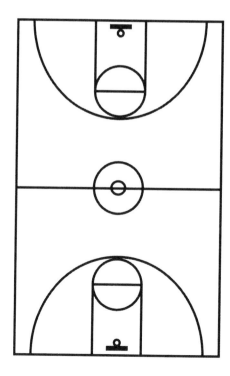

JUMP BALL

Name: _____

Information: _____
_____
_____
_____
_____
_____
_____

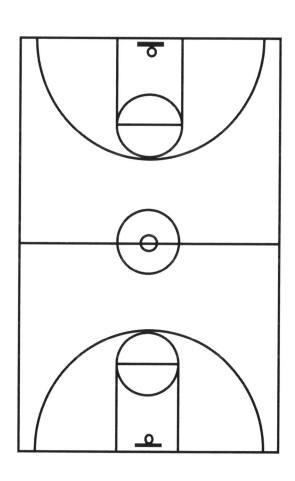